FIGHTBALL

Dying of Suck

Kris Wehrmeister

Printed in the United States of America

First Printing, 2015

ISBN: 978-0692554173

Published by Pretty All True
Lake Oswego, Oregon 97034

www.PrettyAllTrue.com

Dear reader —

My daughters have been kind enough to allow me to use their names in this book, but the telling itself ... is mine.

I am a storyteller of the hyperbolic sort.

Maj and Kallan are free to claim or disavow any and all of my words. Each girl, no matter her position and its possible opposition to the position held by her sister or anyone else in this world, is absolutely correct.

Always.

— Kris

For my daughters, Maj and Kallan. Obviously.

Table of Contents

Fightball: Dying of Suck ...

In the end

It's October in the end.

Sometimes, when you let go, you realize how very little you have been holding. When Mark and I finally uncurl our fingers from what we think is California, all we hold is dusty stubborn pride. We look at one another, and then we speak ... through the truths of our own bitterness and over the mingled late-night sounds of gunshots, fleeing cars, and screaming. After far too long, there is the sound of sirens, wailing the varying notes of neighboring precincts. A search-light helicopter flies above, intermittently filling our living room with the truth of what isn't there.

"So we're leaving?"

"Yes."

Our daughters sleep through the altering of their paths.

Weird, how quiet it can be in the midst of chaos.

First the mom dies

A few weeks later, Mark and I sit down with the girls. I take a deep breath. "We need to talk."

Both girls gaze at me with impossibly huge blue eyes, and ten-year-old Maj reaches for her little sister's hand. "Are you dying?"

I stare at the girls curiously, registering action before words — Why is Maj holding Kallan's hand? Maj doesn't like to touch people, much less hold hands. I cast about in the air for her words, and I am crushed. "What? No, Maj. No." They thought I was dying?

Maj releases eight-year-old Kallan's hand and scrapes her germ-contaminated palm along her pantleg. She looks up at Mark and then back to me. "So is Daddy dying?"

"Sweetie, nobody's dying."

Kallan smiles and nods her head. "That's good, then. We were just wondering."

I can't help myself. "You were just wondering?"

Maj explains, "We knew something was going on. You and Daddy aren't exactly stealthy. We knew something big was coming; we just didn't know what it was."

Kallan nods. "In the movies, the mom always dies. That's pretty much how the adventure gets started — First, the mom says *We have to talk* and then the mom dies and then the fun starts."

I repeat her words, "First the mom dies and then the fun starts?"

Kallan addresses Mark, "Daddy, we didn't really think you were dying, but we didn't want you to feel left out."

Maj nods agreement. "Yeah, mostly we figured Mother would die and then our lives would change."

Kallan explains to me, "It's true, Mom. It's not a bad thing. It's just true. That's why in the movies the mom always has to die. If she lived, no one would ever get to fight space aliens or go in a hot-air balloon or ride dolphins or kill bad guys or find treasure. Because the mom would be all, *Get back here right this instant, young ladies! Get away from those bad guys and step away from that balloon and leave those dolphins alone and who knows what germs those aliens are carrying and this treasure goes right into the lost-and-found where it belongs. It's time to do your homework and take a bath, for goodness sakes.*"

Maj turns to her sister. "OK, but I want to make clear that if I ever do go on an adventure, I am so bringing hand sanitizer."

Kallan nods. "Obviously, Maj. It's not like if Mom died, you would just automatically be normal."

Maj takes offense. "Are you saying I am not normal?"

"Maj, it would take more than Mom dying to straighten you out." Kallan giggles.

I wave my hands. "This whole conversation is annoying me. I do not keep you guys from having adventures. Your lives would not be improved by my death." I turn to Mark. "How am I a woman who just uttered that last sentence to her children? Tell them they would not be better off without me. Tell them adventures are possible even as I continue to clutter up their lives with mothering."

The girls look up at their father expectantly, and he says, "Girls, your mother is all the adventure you will ever need."

I glare at him over our daughters' laughter. "Seriously?"

When the laughter dies down, Maj asks, "So what were we really going to talk about, anyway?"

I am annoyed. "I'm dying, that's what."

Mark reaches to wrap his arm around me. "What your mother means to say is that we are moving. We're going to sell this house, and we're going to move to Oregon."

I sigh. "Yes, that's what I meant to say. We're moving."

Maj raises her hand to stop the conversation. "That was my second guess, after Mother dying. I was like ninety-percent Mother is dying and seven-percent we're moving."

Once again, the conversation is pulled off course as I ask, "What about the other three percent?"

"What?"

"You only explained 97% of your guesses. What about the other three percent?"

Realization dawns. "Oh, the other three percent was that my real parents had finally managed to track you two kidnappers down and had come to whisk me away into my real and way better life."

Kallan nudges her sister. "Ummm … you and I look exactly alike. If you're adopted, so am I."

Maj turns to Kallan. "Duh."

Kallan nods. "OK, that's alright then."

This conversation is not going at all as I expected, but I try to wrench us back on course. "So this is going to be a big change.

You're going to make new friends and you'll be attending a regular school and ..."

Both girls look at me, startled, and Maj speaks, "Wait. We're going to stop home-schooling?"

I nod. "Yes, we were really only doing the home-schooling thing while we tried to find a way out of this school district."

Maj is pleased. "Are we moving somewhere where the schools are good?"

"Yes."

She speaks seriously, "Good, because I think we were just about to reach your teaching limits."

"What are you talking about? I have been doing an awesome job home-schooling you guys."

Maj explains, "Mother, let's just say that you don't always know what you don't know. And, well ...," she shrugs, "It hasn't seemed quite fair that we're expected to just have to take your word for everything."

Incredulous, I defend myself. "Wait just a minute. I have been doing an amazing job at this whole home-schooling thing."

"Mother, we appreciate what you have been doing, but like I said, I think we were about to reach the limits of your knowledge."

"Maj, you are ten. Are you saying my knowledge extends no further than 5th grade?"

Maj ignores me and turns again to her younger sister. "I hope we're not too far behind."

Both girls glare up at me, and I glare back at them. "You are not behind, you idiots. You are way ahead. Geez. Way ahead."

Kallan worries aloud, "What if they put me back in kindergarten?"

"Oh my god, you two are so irritating! Nobody's behind! Stop being so stupid!"

Maj tells on me. "Daddy, Mother is calling us stupid and also she called us idiots and all we are doing is trying to take in the news that we are moving."

Mark nods and speaks mildly, "Your mother knows better than that."

I slump to the floor. "You know what? You three move to Oregon. I'm not coming. You guys don't need me. Pretend I'm dead. Go. Have an adventure. Kiss sea lions and ride in helicopters — I don't even care."

Eyebrows raised, Maj says, "*Someone's* feeling a little dramatic."

Mark speaks again. "It's a lot to take in, I know. Just understand that your mother and I have everything under control."

They stare at him, and he points at me. "It might also interest you to know that this whole adventure? The whole thing — the move and Oregon and new schools and selling the house — all Mommy's idea. I'm totally on board, and I think it will be great, but you should know that the adventure itself? Mommy's idea."

Maj sighs. "So basically, we have put our lives in Mother's whimmish hands? Yeah, Daddy. That sounds like a genius idea."

"Hey! I do not have *whimmish* hands!"

The girls walk to the doorway, where they turn, and then Maj sums up her version of recent developments. "So what we have here are mistakes, bad decisions, running away, adventures while our mother is still alive (which is in violation of every Disney rule in existence), and the promise that our parents — who up until this point in our lives have not had everything under control — have everything under control. There is chaos all around, we're not adopted, and we're probably going to get sweaters and raincoats for Christmas." She looks down at me and clucks false sympathy before asking, "That about the size of it?"

And then we all rest in silence for a moment in the spaces that soon will no longer be ours.

Kallan turns to her sister as they walk away. "Why are we getting raincoats for Christmas?"

Mark stares after them in silence.

They are way too sassy, those girls.

They get that from their father.

I call out after them, "Good talk, girls!"

And we're off.

On an adventure.

This is Maj

We move in January. We spend an entire day supervising the packing of our lives into an enormous moving van, and then the four of us stand in the empty of the house that has been our home for ten years, stunned into silence by the spaces already left behind. We sleep that night on air mattresses, and in the morning, we make final preparations for the ten-hour drive to our new home in Oregon. We need the back seats of the cars to pack the last of our belongings, and so after finding a place for everything but the people, we are left with exactly four seats, two in the front of each car.

Maj is annoyed as she surveys the available seating. "Kallan and I are not even supposed to sit in the front seats. We're too small, and the airbags will decapitate us if you fall asleep and drive into a tree."

Mark is matter-of-fact. "Your mother and I will just be extra careful not to drive while sleeping. Luckily, we have plenty of drugs."

There is a gasp of horror from Maj, and I hurry to reassure her. "He means coffee, Maj. We've got plenty of coffee."

Kallan leans into first one car and then the other. "Where are the dogs going to sit?"

I explain, "They don't need seats; we're just shoving them in. Daddy's carrying all the chemicals and cleaning products and potentially lethal stuff the movers were scared to transport for us, and I will be driving all the pets."

"Wait, so one of us gets all the pets?"

I gesture at the back of the minivan, indicating the covered (but air-holed) tanks in which I have housed the turtles and the frogs and the fish. "These guys are all safe and warm back here, and the dogs are going to sit on the floor of the back-seat area."

Maj protests, "Why can't we each take one of the dogs?"

Kallan knows. "Because whichever dog rides with the chemicals and lethal stuff will be dead when we get there. Maj, our dogs are dumb."

Maj nods. "This is true. Fine, so which one of us rides with lethal toxicity?"

"I'll take the death chemicals, you take the lethal toxicity, Maj."

"Kallan, that doesn't even make ...," Maj pauses as realization dawns, and she turns to me, "Awww, man ... that means I get the farter."

Hands on my hips, I feign annoyance. "I do not even fart that much."

"Not you, Mother. Obviously." She turns to glare at Persie the Labrador, who tip tip tips her tail in advance apology. "Listen up, Lab ... I don't care if you're a balloon when we get there, you hear me? Hold those farts for the duration of the trip."

I grab Jack the Lakeland Terrier, who counts flatulence as one of the only bad qualities he does not possess, and I lie, "Come on, Maj. The dogs will be fine."

Maj sighs heavily and reaches to scratch Jack behind the ears. "You better be a good dog."

Kallan hops into Mark's car, delighted to be dog-free. "Alright, let's get going. Oregon, here we come!"

I open the sliding minivan door and shove the dogs into the small remaining back-seat spaces. "Hop in, Maj."

Maj yells at her sister, "Make sure your phone is turned on! I'm going to text you! I'm going to call you! Be prepared!" Kallan holds her phone aloft in acknowledgment, and Maj climbs in the minivan, buckling her seatbelt as I start up the car. "It's good you got us these phones, Mother. This way, Kallan and I can be in constant communication during this drive of sisterly separation."

I follow Mark out of the driveway and out of our neighborhood, and Maj texts her sister, narrating her texts for me as she types. "I'm asking Kallan what she is going to do during this long boring drive."

There is a moment of silence and then Maj yells loudly enough that a startle-loosed Labrador fart fills the car. **"SHE SAYS SHE IS GOING TO WATCH MOVIES THE WHOLE TRIP! MOTHER, HOW IS SHE WATCHING MOVIES? OH MY GOSH, WE ARE BEING GASSED TO POO-DOOM! OPEN A WINDOW! HOW IS SHE WATCHING MOVIES?"**

I crack a window, apologizing as I do. "I can't open the window all the way. Jack will jump out and be flattened to terrier roadkill."

She texts furiously. "I'm informing that child she may not watch movies the entire trip. Ten hours of movies is insanity! How does she even have the ability to watch movies, anyway?"

"I think she has the portable DVD player."

"YOU THINK, MOTHER? YOU THINK? RESPONSIBLE PARENTING INVOLVES ACTUAL KNOWLEDGE!"

"Listen, Maj. You hate watching movies, in the car or out. It's not like you're missing out on something you want to do. Who cares if she watches movies? She's happy. Daddy's happy. Especially if Kallan uses the earphones, because then he can listen to his own music. They're fine."

Maj reads aloud the response text from her sister, her voice shrill with incredulity. **"SHE SAYS SHE IS WATCHING MOVIES UNTIL SHE ARRIVES AT HER NEW HOUSE. SHE SAYS SHE PLUGGED IT INTO THE CIGARETTE LIGHTER AND SHE CAN WATCH SHOWS UNTIL WE HIT A TREE! AND SHE IS EATING PRINGLES AND DOUGHNUTS! SHE SAYS DADDY SAYS THIS IS A NO-RULES RIDE! DADDY HAS GONE OFF THE RAILS AND WE HAVEN'T EVEN GOTTEN ON THE FREEWAY YET!"**

"Maj, calm down."

She texts her sister bossy directions about snacks and nutrition, but the response from Kallan must be unsatisfactory in the extreme, because Maj's next directions are to me. **"MOTHER, I DEMAND THAT YOU RUN THEM OFF THE ROAD RIGHT THIS INSTANT! WE NEED TO TALK SOME SENSE INTO THEM!"**

I reach down and beside my seat, pop open the circular tube I find there. "You want some Pringles?"

"IT IS 7:30 IN THE MORNING, MOTHER! SENSIBLE PEOPLE DO NOT EAT PRINGLES IN THE DAWN, MOTHER!"

The dogs, unburdened by the requirements of peopleness or sense, smell the Pringles and go insane. Jack leaps to the front of the car and burrows wildly. I reach to toss him back once, twice, three times. "Geez, we're going to have to hogtie Jack." I throw him back a fourth time, and this time he lands on Persie's eagerly curious head, and the larger dog farts in terror.

Maj waves her hands to clear the air. "This is the worst drive ever. How long until we get there?"

I glance at the clock. "About nine hours and 54 minutes."

She is texting again. "I'm telling Kallan that I am going to call her and inform her of the rules of road-trips."

"Seriously, Maj?"

"SOMEONE HAS TO PARENT THAT GIRL! SHE HAS JUMPED INTO THE CHAOS CHASM! THERE ARE RULES! THERE ARE RULES BY WHICH PEOPLE ABIDE. SHE NEEDS TO ABIDE OR DIE." Her thumbs tap out the message. "I'm telling her that she needs to check in with me for the rules. I'm telling her you said to pick up the phone or you will punish her harshly." She types out the last two words. "M-O-T-H-E-R S-A-I-D," and she turns to me. "There. That should get her attention."

I sigh. "Those rules of which you spoke. The ones for road-trips — any chance one of the rules is mind your own business? Any chance another rule might be no screaming in the car?"

She ignores me, instead staring at her phone, awaiting a response, and then she waves her phone angrily in front of my face. **"OH, THIS IS NOT OK. KALLAN SAYS, AND THIS IS A QUOTE … 'MAJ, YOU ARE NOT THE BOSS OF ME.'"**

"She has a point."

"AND NOW SHE IS TEXTING ME THAT SHE IS TURNING HER PHONE OFF! SHE SAYS I AM DISTRACTING HER FROM HER SHOWS! SHE SAYS SHE IS EATING A SECOND DOUGHNUT! SHE SAYS DADDY PROMISED HER HOT CHOCOLATE!"

"Maj, seriously … calm down and do your own life for a bit."

"AND NOW SHE ISN'T ANSWERING MY TEXTS!" Maj stabs at her phone and leaves a voice message. **"LISTEN, YOUNG LADY. TURN YOUR PHONE BACK ON RIGHT THIS INSTANT AND DEAL WITH ME! CALL ME BACK."** As a seeming afterthought, she adds, "This is Maj," and hangs up.

She makes five more phone calls in rapid succession ...

"**KALLAN, CALL ME BACK. I HAVE SOMETHING IMPORTANT TO TELL YOU.** This is Maj."

"**KALLAN, THERE IS PERIL ALL AROUND! CALL ME BACK. IT'S AN EMERGENCY.** This is Maj."

"**KALLAN, WHEN WE GET TO THE FIRST REST-STOP, I AM GOING TO POUND YOU INTO BREAD DOUGH.** This is Maj."

"**KALLAN, YOU APPEAR TO BE UNCLEAR ON THE ETIQUETTE OF PHONE MESSAGES. CALL ME BACK.** This is Maj."

"**KALLAN, I THINK YOUR PHONE MIGHT BE BROKEN. CALL ME BACK.** This is Maj."

I grab for Maj's phone. "Sweetie, stop. Call one of your friends instead."

"Eh. Tired of saying goodbye. Besides, they're all still sleeping."

"OK, well ... leave Kallan alone. Talk to me. I'm right here. We have a long day ahead of us, just you and me ... talk to me."

She bounces huffily in her seat for a few minutes, and then she takes a deep breath. "Can I ask you a question?"

"Sure."

"You said that when we moved to Vallejo ten years ago, you and Daddy thought the city was going to get better, right?"

"Yes, a lot of people were moving to Vallejo at the time. It seemed as though the city was turning around."

"So you spent that first few years devoting all your time and money to remodeling our house."

"Because we planned to live there forever. We loved that house."

"But then when I got old enough to go to school, the schools were terrible, and so I went to private school; and then two years later, Kallan joined me."

"True."

"A lot of our friends moved away."

"True."

"And then things got bad at the private school, and you pulled us out to home-school."

"So far, this is an accurate summary of events. Is there a question in here somewhere?"

"And you spent more money on the house, and more friends moved away."

I say nothing.

"And the city did not get better; it just kept getting worse."

Sigh.

"And then the city went bankrupt."

"Yup."

"And then the city got scarier and scarier."

"Yup."

"And more of our friends moved away."

"You are making me sad."

"And then all the houses started having foreclosure signs in front of them."

"Yeah."

"And still we stayed."

"Yes."

"And there were almost no police or ambulances or firemen because of the bankruptcy."

"Yeah."

"And still we stayed. We made new friends and we stayed."

"Yeah ... what exactly is your question?"

"But now we're leaving."

"Yes."

"Because it's time."

"Yes."

She sighs. "So I guess my question is, if you had to do it all over again, would you have moved to Vallejo in the first place?"

"Honestly? No."

"Follow-up question, then — Don't you and Daddy feel pretty stupid for staying as long as you did? For making our family stay there as long as you did? I mean, when you list out the truths of our time in Vallejo — Don't you and Daddy feel pretty stupid?"

Stupid and heartbroken, but I don't say that. Instead I say, "Sometimes, it takes bad decisions and bad results to make you see what it is you really want. It's hard to admit failure. Your father and I are stubborn people. We wanted things to work out."

"But things didn't work out."

"Nope. They did not."

"And Oregon will be better?"

"Yes."

"How do you know?"

"I just do."

Maj sighs. "That is not a satisfactory answer."

"Trust me."

"Mother, it's like you don't even know me." She glances over at the speedometer. "**MOTHER, YOU ARE GOING 65 MILES AN HOUR!**"

"That's the speed limit, Maj. Besides, I'm following Daddy - I don't want to lose him."

"**SPEED LIMITS ARE THE MAXIMUM ALLOWABLE SPEED, MOTHER! YOU DO NOT HAVE TO HIT THE MAXIMUM TO MAKE PROGRESS! SLOW DOWN TO ACCOUNT FOR CONDITIONS AND MAKE DADDY MATCH YOUR PACE!**"

"What conditions?"

"What conditions, Mother? Are you kidding me? What about the fact **THAT I AM IN THE CAR AND I AM DEMANDING THE BRAKES BE APPLIED?**"

"Maj, this is going to be the longest day and the longest drive in the history of the world."

She glances at the speedometer again. "Now we are going 68 miles per hour. How am I supposed to trust you with the rest of my life if I cannot even trust you from moment to moment as we flee down the highway?"

"We are not fleeing. Seriously, Maj ... take some deep breaths. Trust me. Everything is going to be alright."

There is a moment of silence into which Maj does not breathe deeply, and then she starts a new topic. "If my frogs die, I am going to bury them with the trust that died with them."

"Your frogs are fine."

"Mother, you are not attuned to the frogs like I am. They are not fine. They are terrified and they are breathing in the toxins of what they believe to be the end of the world through the permeable membranes of their skin. Frogs hate change. Frogs let change poison them."

"Good thing you're not a frog, then."

"Mother, did you just acknowledge that the frogs are going to die?"

"I said no such thing. The frogs will be fine. I packed them in a warmed cooler with moss and water and hiding places. They will be fine. You can check on them when we stop along the way."

She turns to yell into the back of the car, "Listen up, men of rubber. You have been with me a long time, and so **TRUST WHAT I SAY** — this is not the end of the world. Tomorrow will arrive and things will be OK. Do you hear me, men of rubber? **DO NOT DIE.** That smell you are absorbing through your body is not the end of the world, it is only dog flatulence."

And the Labrador farts again.

"PERSIE, STOP FARTING DOOM ON THE FROGS! YOU ARE SCARING THEM! YOU ARE MAKING THEM BREATHE POO FRAGMENTS! STOP IT RIGHT THIS INSTANT!" She turns to me, nose held tightly. "Did you know that farts are actually airborne bits of fecal matter?"

"Yes, I did know that."

"Do farts kill frogs?"

Before I can answer, one of the frogs starts croaking a response, a loud throaty dog-bark of a sound that fills the car and puts both actual dogs on high alert. As the frog keeps talking, Jack the terrier starts scaling the mountain of belongings separating him from the frogs, and Maj leans back to grab him. "Get back here, stupid terrier. I will tie you to the front bumper if you eat my frogs." She presses Jack down into her lap, where he struggles and kicks for freedom as the frog winds down its soliloquy and a panicky Persie farts again.

I roll the window down a bit more and gasp for air. "Seriously, this is going to be the longest day in the history of the world."

Maj works to leash Jack as she moves to the next topic. "So the short-sale thing ... what exactly does that mean?"

"Maj, you are ten."

"What's your point, Mother?"

"Trust your daddy and me with the grown-up stuff. You be ten."

"This IS me being ten, and I am going to assume from your non-answer that the short-sale thing is very bad indeed."

I hand Maj her phone. "Here. Maybe your sister turned her phone back on."

She tries. "Nope. She is ignoring me."

"Text Daddy, then."

"MOTHER, DADDY IS NOT ALLOWED TO TEXT WHILE DRIVING."

"No, I meant text Daddy to tell him Kallan has to turn her phone back on."

"Oh!" She presses buttons. "Good idea."

I reach to turn the radio on. Maj does not look up from her phone as she directs me, "OK, but maximum volume is 15 and I pick the stations and no singing and no clapping **BECAUSE HANDS ON THE WHEEL** and also no commercials and no countdowns because those are stupid and no inappropriate lyrics **BECAUSE I AM AN IMPRESSIONABLE CHILD, MOTHER.**"

I glance at the clock, which reads 8:05. "Tell Daddy I am going to need more coffee."

She glances sideways at me. "I thought you had plenty of coffee."

"Just tell him."

She waits for a response, which she then reads to me. "Daddy says Kallan says her phone is broken and he has the Benadryl in his car if we need some." She texts furiously, narrating as she goes, "**DADDY, YOU MAY NOT DRUG YOUR CHILDREN! ALSO STOP TEXTING WITH ME BEFORE YOU ARE DOUSED WITH ACID AND YOUR SKIN IS BOILED OFF!**"

I think for a moment. "Oh, because he's carrying the chemicals." I snort with laughter.

Maj glares at me. "I know the two of you well enough to know that the chemicals Daddy is carrying are probably poured into flimsy Ziploc bags, just waiting for a small accident to release them from their fair-fish baggies and hurl them toward the prize of melty skin. Also, drugging your child is not funny, Mother. **I AM ONTO YOU AND I WILL BE ON HIGH ALERT FOR TAMPERING OF FOOD AND BEVERAGES DURING THIS TRIP.**" She huffs. "Wait until we get to the state border and they start asking questions about your mothering ... I guess we'll see who's laughing then." She pets Jack, who has surrendered to sleep in the warmth of her lap. "Yes, wait until we get to the mothering checkpoint. Just you wait."

I reach to pat her leg. "Maj, it's so cute how you think I will stop at a checkpoint and submit to questioning." I reach to tug at her seatbelt. "Good — you'll want to be securely positioned when the ramming begins."

"Mother, if you won't answer to the actual authorities, then **YOU WILL ANSWER TO ME.**"

"OK, but seriously ... I am going to need more coffee."

"You just had coffee."

"I need more. Also, I need to use the bathroom."

"Already? At some point, you might want to think about owning the truths of your addiction, Mother."

"OK, so text Daddy. We need coffee, a bathroom, and a muzzle."

"What? I don't think we need to muzzle the dogs, Mother. They're behaving — the car seems to be making them sleepy, and so why would we go to the trouble of muzzling — **OH MY GOSH, MOTHER ... YOU DON'T MEAN FOR THE DOGS, DO YOU? THIS IS EXACTLY THE SORT OF THING I PLAN TO BRING UP AT THE MOTHERING CHECKPOINT.**"

The clock reads 8:17.

Coffee.

Definitely.

Men of rubber

"Mother, wake up. Decisions are required, and Daddy says he wants nothing to do with us."

I do not open my eyes. "Why does Daddy get to wash his hands of you?"

Maj's voice is matter-of-fact. "Daddy said he knew you would say that, and he says to tell you that he is not in the mood for us and so you get us and also he says he is making coffee by way of apology."

I open my eyes; both girls are kneeling on the floor beside my head, their eyes huge and blue, their faces tense with readiness for the debate they need me to referee. I stretch and throw the covers aside; my whole body aches; the air mattress appears to have sprung a leak, and I am too old to sleep on the floor. Sadly, our furniture won't be here for a few days. I sigh and then inhale deeply of the scent of brewing coffee. "Let me guess ... bedroom assignments?" The girls nod, anxious to begin the conflict. I pull the blankets back up around my chin. "Any chance we can resolve this without me getting out of bed?"

"Mother, technically you are on the living-room floor," Maj points out.

Kallan yanks on my blankets. "Come on, Mom. Don't you want to see the house in the light? Don't you want to see what your children look and sound like in their new house?"

Maj turns to her sister. "We look and sound like we always look and sound. Arguing here sounds like arguing everywhere we go. Why are you getting her hopes up?"

I reach for the jumble of clothes on the floor beside me and pull on a T-shirt and jeans. After running smoothing fingers through my hair, I glance over at the tanks that hold the turtle and frogs and fish. "You guys check on them? They seem OK?"

"The fish aren't belly-floating, and I think that's as close to a thumbs-up as we are going to get from them." Maj sprinkles a bit of food into their tank, and the fish gobble to the surface. "They seem fine."

Kallan walks to her turtle's tank. "Delilah will feel a lot better about things when she gets settled in her new room. She doesn't like to be on the floor where dogs might peel her out of her shell like a hard-boiled egg."

Maj hovers over the tank that holds her frogs. "Little is fine, but Big looks weird."

"Big always looks weird, Maj." Kallan reassures her sister, "Ever since he let that stick poke his eye out, he always looks weird. Paranoid and weird."

Maj shakes her head. "No, this is different. This looks like surrender." She leans in to yell at her frogs, "Listen up, men of rubber! I did not bring you all the way to Oregon for you to die. Yes, I get it ... the move was scary ... blah blah blah. Bookmark the terror and turn the page, frog-boys, because death is not an option!" She directs her next words to the smaller handicapped frog. "Listen up, one-eyed Big, take a single-dimensioned look around and **DEAL WITH YOUR NEW LIFE! THIS IS YOUR NEW HOME AND YOU WILL NOT CLOSE YOUR REMAINING EYE, DO YOU HEAR ME? YOU WILL NOT! THIS IS MAJ SPEAKING AND I WILL NOT BE DEALT A HAND OF RUBBERED DEATH!**"

I stare at her. "Way to pep-talk the frogs, Maj."

She stands. "Being a pet owner comes with certain responsibilities, Mother."

Kallan giggles. "That reminds me. Mom, call Persie."

"Why?"

Both girls are giggling now, and Maj urges me to cooperate, "Just do it, Mother."

Puzzled, I call for the Labrador, "Persie! Come here, Persie!"

Mark responds from the other room, "Give her a minute. She's coming."

The girls walk to stand on either side of me, and we watch as the Labrador enters the room. Something is obviously wrong ... the dog moves like a fat legless sea lion; she undulates across the floor toward us, her eyes rolling in terror, her head pressed to the ground. Her chubby body inchworm-ripples with every undulation; everything about the dog is tragic and forlorn. I stare as the Labrador arrives and rolls against my feet, having traversed the entire length of the room without using her legs. I bend to pet her head. "What on earth is wrong with Persie? Why isn't she walking?"

The girls giggle hysterically, and Kallan explains, "She's not hurt. She just seems to be afraid that the new house is going to cave in on her, and so she is making herself as small as possible."

I examine each of Persie's feet. "You sure she's not hurt?"

"Watch, Mother." Maj and Kallan kneel behind the dog, and working together, they shove the Labrador across the hardwood floor into the kitchen and then across that floor as well. I follow behind; Persie allows herself, her eyes rolling skyward, to be slid across the house as though this is the new normal. The girls, still on their knees, look up from their Labrador-shaped curling stone, and Maj says again, "Watch, Mother." Kallan stands to pull open the door that accesses the back yard, and Maj gives the dog a final great push. As soon as Persie's toes meet the threshold of the sliding-glass door, she leaps into the air and hurls herself out into the back yard, where she runs happily across the expanse of lawn, using all four legs.

The girls shriek with laughter, and Mark hands me a cup of coffee, observing, "Persie is not completely on-board with the new house."

He's holding Jack the terrier in the crook of his arm, and I suggest, "You want to toss him in the back yard as well?"

"No, I went out to have a look at the fence, and although it encloses the yard, there are places for Jack to easily fit beneath it." Mark sighs, clearly frustrated at the thought of having to do battle with our stubborn escapist terrier. "Maybe chicken-wire along the bottom of the fence."

That seems like a lot of work, so I say, "Hold off on the chicken-wire; I might have a better idea." I sip at my coffee, and I gesture at the riotously patterned backsplash of our new rental-house kitchen. "Good lord … it was ugly in the photos, but it's worse in person. What were they thinking?"

Mark runs his fingers along the backsplash. "I believe they were thinking, *What an amazing deal we got on this hideous tile for the house in which we will no longer reside!*"

"Seriously."

Maj and Kallan return their attention to me, and Kallan says, "OK, Mom … about the bedroom assignments." Reluctantly, I follow the girls upstairs, where the issue is immediately apparent: one of the bedrooms is slightly larger than the other.

Maj leaps ahead to position herself squarely in the middle of the larger bedroom, the windows of which look out onto the back yard. "Alright, my thinking is that I am older and so I get the bigger bedroom. The end. Case closed."

Kallan head-butts her sister out of the middle of the room and turns to me. "And my thinking is that I should get the bigger room because all Maj does in her room is be Maj, and I need space for dancing and gymnastics and trouble-causing."

I look around. This larger room is painted in strident shades of blue and green ... blue for sky and green for the hills, backdrop for an all-encompassing stenciled set of train tracks on which run a variety of stenciled trains. "Are there stencils in the other bedroom as well?"

Kallan nods. "Zoo animals, but pastels and not so overwhelming."

We walk across the hall to the smaller room. The windows in this room look out on the front of the house with an additional window that opens out over the roof of the garage. The stenciling in this light-blue room is much less obtrusive. I run my fingers over the shape of a small yellow rabbit. "A couple of posters and some double-sided tape, and this room goes from baby boy to third-grade girl in a matter of moments. The other room is always going to be a train room."

Maj holds up a hand. "Wait just a minute. Why wouldn't we just paint over the trains?"

I explain, "The thing about renting is that we're not going to be spending time and money on cosmetic changes."

"I'M JUST SUPPOSED TO LIVE AND SLEEP AMONGST THE DEMON TRAINS?"

Kallan is already opening the window that allows access onto the garage. "Check it out! I could totally walk out onto the roof and escape from the house any time I want!"

"MOTHER, I HAVE CHANGED MY MIND. I LIKE THIS ROOM BETTER ... I DEMAND THAT I BE GIVEN THE ROOM THAT ALLOWS ESCAPE!"

Kallan shakes her head as she starts to climb out the window. "Too late, Maj. You live with the cheerful ghost trains of death."

"I REFUSE TO LIVE WITH THE CHEERFUL GHOST TRAINS OF DEATH!"

Kallan is casually supportive from out on the garage roof. "Maj, it's not like the trains of death will be coming for you as you sleep ... probably."

"I CANNOT SLEEP BENEATH THE RAILED THREAT OF DEATH TRANSPORT! MOTHER, WHAT DO YOU NOT COMPREHEND ABOUT MY DEMANDS AND PROTESTATIONS?"

I turn to look at her. "What's this *Mother* thing, anyway? I've noticed it recently ... is that permanent?"

Maj is startled by the change in topic, and she abandons her screaming. "What? Yes, I have decided to start calling you *Mother*. I'm too old to call you *Mom* or *Mommy*."

"Awww ... I like when you call me *Mommy*."

"Tough. I'm done with that."

"Bummer."

"Also, Mother? I am thinking that if I refer to you as *Mother*, your attention will be drawn to the actual job of mothering, a job that is yours and which you too often let go unattended, especially where Kallan is concerned. That child needs parenting, Mother. **SHE IS OUT ON THE ROOF AT THIS VERY MOMENT, MOTHER! PERHAPS YOU MIGHT WANT TO CONSIDER RUSTLING UP SOME MOTHERING TO IMPOSE ON THAT GIRL!**"

Kallan reappears at the window, sticks her head in. "This is going to be awesome! Anytime I want, I can just disappear!"

"MOTHER, I DEMAND THAT YOU PARENT THAT CHILD INTO PERMANENCE."

"Look, Maj!" Kallan walks away from the window, onto the garage roof and out of sight. "Maj, seriously ... this is like a dream come true!"

"MOTHER, PUT A STOP TO THE DREAMS OF DISAPPEARANCE!"

I take that as my cue, and I step out of the room and head back downstairs, where I find Mark. He looks up from the folder of rental-agreement paperwork. "You get the girls settled into bedrooms?"

I shake my head. "Settled? Never. But we did agree that Maj will take the room on the back of the house, so as to better muffle her over-the-top **BOLDED CAPITAL-LETTERED** voice."

He laughs. "You told her that?"

"No ... it just worked out that way, thank goodness ... also, Kallan is out on the garage roof."

"Of course she is."

I look around for the terrier. "Where's Jack?"

"Last I saw, he was headed for the basement ... something down there smells like death, and he's playing detective."

"Well, that's awesome news."

"Right?"

The girls reappear, and Maj announces, "Kallan and I have been through the entire house, and we are of the opinion that this is a serious downgrade from our previous circumstances."

Kallan puts up a hesitant finger. "Although I am willing to be more enthusiastic if you'll agree to put a pool in the back yard."

I laugh. "A pool?"

"It's plenty big enough ... look!" Kallan points out at the large green yard. "There's plenty of room!" She and her sister look at me expectantly.

I drain my coffee cup. "Perhaps we should go over the whole rental-house concept again."

Kallan sighs. "So no pool?"

"When our furniture arrives, somewhere in the moving van is a small plastic wading pool ... I'm sure the dogs will share."

Maj is unexpectedly cheerful, and she turns to her sister. "It's not that big a deal. This is our temporary rental house. We won't be here for long. When we buy a house, we'll just make sure there's a pool."

"Even though this house is temporary, you might want to adjust your definition of temporary," Mark suggests gently.

Maj glares at him. "How big do I have to stretch the word *temporary*?"

Mark shrugs. "A year? Maybe two?"

"A FIFTH OF THE LIFE I HAVE LIVED SO FAR? IS THAT WHAT YOU ARE SAYING? ARE YOU KIDDING ME RIGHT NOW?"

"Maybe less, but we're not in a position to buy another house right now."

The girls consider this news, and then Kallan asks, "But I thought we were selling our house in Vallejo. Just use the money you get from that to buy a new house."

"Yeah, about that." Mark pauses. "We're probably going to lose money on that deal. Things are a little up in the air until we get a handle on exactly where we stand."

"WHY DON'T WE KNOW WHERE WE STAND, DADDY? HOW COULD YOU ALLOW US TO STAND IF WE DON'T KNOW WHERE WE ARE STANDING?"

"Well," Mark explains, "I need to find a job."

Maj is aghast. **"YOU DON'T HAVE A JOB?"**

He continues, "At the moment, neither your mother nor I have jobs, and so … we're not sure when we're going to have enough money to buy a house again."

"WE DON'T HAVE ANY MONEY?"

"Well, it turns out no one wants to buy our Vallejo house at the price we owe on it, and so …"

"WE'RE GOING TO BE POOR?"

"Not poor. Careful."

Kallan voice is more wail than words. "But I don't want to be careful!"

Mark tries again, "The thing is, sometimes in life, you have to make a decision — Do I stay here in the unhappy known or do I travel toward the possibly happy unknown?"

Maj clutches at her chest. **"YOU KNOW I HATE UNKNOWN! THIS SOUNDS VERY BAD, DADDY."**

Kallan agrees. "It kind of does, Daddy."

Mark and I are saved from further explanations, because into this moment runs a small terrier with a very dead and very smelly rat-corpse clutched in his teeth.

A good omen.

All the possible lies

"Can we use your travel mugs?" The girls stand in the kitchen and look at me hopefully.

I reach for the mugs, unscrew the tops, rinse them out. "What do you need them for?"

"We're just doing a bit of collecting in the back yard," Maj explains, "and we don't have any plastic bowls or anything."

"Yeah," adds Kallan, "Did you know there's a pretty big fruit and vegetable garden at the very back of the yard? Even though it's January, there's some stuff growing."

I rest the travel mugs on the counter, wishing I had thought to pack a few dishes in one of the cars ... who knows when the movers will get here? "Well, harvest what you can, because you know my history with gardens."

"Mother, won't the owners of the house care if you kill their garden?"

I hesitate before answering. "I may have assured them that your father and I love gardening."

Maj is concerned. "That is a total lie, Mother."

"It's not a lie if they believe it."

"THAT IS NOT HOW THE SAYING GOES, MOTHER!"

"Whatever."

Her face grows thoughtful. "What else did you lie about, Mother?"

"I may have included a few small untruths in the story of us ... and I may have neglected to say a few other things."

"THAT'S CALLED LYING OMITTING, MOTHER! I WILL NOT STAND FOR THE OMITTING OF LIES!"

"No, that would mean I left out the lies, and I definitely included some lies. You mean *lying by omission*, because I left out important information. And yes ... I did that."

"FINE! I WILL NOT STAND FOR THE OMISSIONING OF LIES!"

"Whatevs."

"WHATEVS IS NOT A WORD, MOTHER. YOU ARE A HOME-SCHOOL PARENT-EDUCATOR! THERE ARE STANDARDS!"

"Actually, I am no longer a home-school educator, so I am officially allowed to speak as ridiculously as I want."

"YOU MAY NOT SPEAK TO ME OF WHATEVS, MOTHER."

"Whatevs."

"Speaking of home-schooling," Kallan reaches into her pocket for a piece of paper, which she begins to unfold as she asks, "When are we going to start real school?"

"Actually, I told another tiny lie about the official end of your home-schooling, and so you have almost two weeks of vacation before you start at your new school."

Kallan is delighted. "That's awesome! Thank you!"

Maj glowers at me. "This is completely unacceptable news."

Kallan hands me the paper she has unfolded. "Before we start real school, I'm going to need some more red crayons."

Her sister reaches for the paper, examines it. "Oh my gosh, Kallan ... it's like your drawing exploded in blood!"

"History is bloody, Maj." Kallan turns to me gleefully and holds up the picture. "It's rack torture. See? The table and wheels are under the blood and body parts, but you can see the outlines."

"Very nice drawing. Very ... ummm ... visceral."

"Kallan, you are not normal. You know that, right? Mother, tell her she's not normal."

Kallan doesn't respond to her sister, but instead casually swipes her fingers across the sheet of paper. "I'm not normal, Maj? *I'm* not normal?"

Maj grits her teeth and squeezes shut her eyes. "Mother, tell her to stop caressing paper. I hate the sound of paper being caressed. It hurts my head."

Kallan lifts her hands and claps three loud times. "How about if I clap?"

"YOU KNOW I CANNOT STAND PERCUSSIVE NONSENSE!"

"How about if I hug you?"

"HUG ME AND DIE, SMALL WOMAN!"

"What if I lick my finger?"

"AIIIEIEIEIEIEIEIEIEIEIEIEE!"

"What if I whistle?"

"MOTHER, KALLAN IS BEING DEMONIC! BRING HER SATANICITY UNDER CONTROL RIGHT THIS INSTANT!"

Kallan raises her eyebrows. "Yeah, Maj ... I'm the one who's not normal."

Maj shudders and takes a deep breath. "Back to you, Mother ... back to the lies you told in order to get us this house."

"Maj, think about it," Kallan says, "Obviously, Mom had to make us look good. Of course she had to lie."

Maj shakes her head. "I can't believe we lied our way into this house. Mother, this is all just a scandal waiting to happen."

Kallan sighs. "Maj, do you know how very bad this family would be at camping?"

"What?"

"Maj, nobody would rent to the truth of us. Even I know that. The truth makes us campers." She turns to me. "Right, Mom?"

I pretend to ponder the question. "Well, let's see. I could have written something like ..." and I turn to type quickly on my laptop as the girls watch the words appear on the screen:

Mark is a responsible and highly accomplished citizen who will be unemployed but hopeful as we enter into this rental agreement. Mark has a goofy sense of humor, a weird tendency toward malapropism, and an interest in craft beer that borders on obsession. Mark will assure others that he enjoys gardening, but in fact he does not. At all.

Kallan bursts into laughter. "Those are all true things!"

I keep typing.

Kris is wildly intelligent, overeducated, and under-accomplished. Kris is incredibly skilled at finding opportunities to render her services in whatever capacity for zero recompense, and so in all likelihood will not be contributing in any meaningful fashion to the payment of rent. She is a competent home-school educator through grade-five materials, the notable exceptions being sarcasm and hostile judgment, subjects in which her students excel far beyond their years. She does not enjoy small talk, and invariably manages to either insult or offend in its execution. She has killed every plant ever entrusted to her care, including cacti.

Kallan points. "Hey, that sounds like you're saying Maj and I are gifted at sarcasm and hostility."

"What's your point, babe?"

Maj snorts and points to the sentence about small talk. "Remember that time you told that woman her hair reminded you of a picture you once saw of a dead person?"

I keep typing. "OK, but in my defense? The dead woman's hair was gorgeous."

Ten-year-old beautiful shortish germ-phobic Maj is smart, opinionated, and consumed with the need for things to be fair. She spends a good portion of her time pointing out the ways in which life is proving not to be fair, with an emphasis on how her mother has failed to ensure the equitable treatment of Maj and her younger sister. To this end, Maj spends a lot of time telling on her sister for real and imagined misdeeds of the mostly unimportant variety. Maj adores rules and structure and reliably handed-down consequences. She is an exceptional student, but she is the sort to remind the teacher that homework has not yet been assigned, and she does not suffer fools lightly. Or heavily. Or at all. Maj is prickly and quirky and demanding and she has a low tolerance for any sort of irritation, which, having been noticed, grows in its assaultive strength until Maj completely loses control and becomes a whirling dervish of ear-shattering hostility and anguish. In the best of times, Maj tends to speak at top-volume, and she has a fearsome and easily triggered temper. Also, she likes frogs.

Maj reads over my shoulder. "A whirling dervish of hostility and anger? Mother, I do not whirl."

Kallan agrees. "It's actually more like her head spins while the rest of her just swells and flails. Mom, you should highlight the word **quirky**. I'm not sure people will understand just how much that word holds in its meaning."

Maj stabs a testy finger at the screen. "*Shortish*, Mother? I am not shortish."

Kallan presses herself up against her sister and brings a measuring hand up to the top of her sister's head. "Well, you're two years older than I am, and I'm not tall, and you are shorter than I am. I would say you are definitely shortish."

"Hmmph."

Eight-year-old beautiful Kallan has recently been studying World History, with a strange and intense focus on the various and unusual ways in which people throughout history have died. Many red crayons are required. She is brilliant in the things that fascinate her and a bit lazy in the things that do not. She is very bad about following rules and telling the truth, and she has a tendency to get herself into trouble just for the entertainment of the trouble. To this end, Kallan enjoys antagonizing her sister to an unhealthy degree. Kallan is imaginative and creative and she has a gift for storytelling. She is wildly funny, and she can do uncanny and generally insulting impressions of the people who matter to her. Kallan is emotional and empathetic and one time she peed her initials on her sister's carpeted bedroom floor but I'm sure that was a one-time deal and will not be a problem in this rental house. Tantrums and angry yelling of the sort that make neighbors peer nervously out of their windows are part of Kallan's everyday repertoire.

Maj huffs angrily. "Kallan better not pee her initials in my new room."

Kallan smiles at the memory. "I've got skills."

Larger fat dog Persie is a Labrador. She eats poo. She is obscenely flatulent. She sheds a lot and she refuses to allow us to cut her toenails, so she clicks when she walks. I'm sure this will not be a hardwood-floor issue, as small gouges and scratches add character to wood.

"That last thing may not actually be an issue if Persie continues flopping around the house without using her legs," Maj observes.

Smaller badly behaved dog Jack is a Lakeland Terrier. Jack is rampantly disobedient with respect to all possible rules a dog might be expected to follow and he has a tendency toward destruction of personal property that may conceal treats, including backpacks, purses, cupboards, boxes of any sort, and shoes. Also, he barks at everything. Loudly. Insistently. Ceaselessly.

Bowl of nameless Beta fish — nothing of interest to report.

Larger single goldfish named Snack lives with the turtle until the turtle figures out the import of Snack's name.

Turtle Delilah lives in a large aquarium and fills her water with turtle poo because that's the only kind she knows how to make.

Two Australian Tree Frogs named Big and Little live in a separate and sometimes smelly terrarium, where they eat live crickets and attract small pesky flies by the millions.

When I have finished typing, Maj sighs. "Alright, the truth would have made us campers. So what did you actually say?"

"I said we are a quiet and respectable family of four that enjoys board games and gardening. We have two exceptionally well-trained dogs. We are in the midst of selling our house and we are looking to rent as we relocate from California to Oregon. The end."

Kallan snorts with laughter. "SERIOUSLY?"

Maj is incredulous. **"NONE OF THAT IS ALL THE WAY TRUE. YOU TOLD ALL THE POSSIBLE LIES!"**

"It's not a lie if they believe it."

"THAT IS NOT HOW THE SAYING GOES, MOTHER!"

"Camping would be very bad, Maj."

She considers and then relents. "This is true."

"OK, then ... next topic ... back-yard collecting." I slide the travel mugs across the counter. "Here."

Kallan reaches for the travel mugs, hands one to her sister, and then she turns back to me. "Can we have the tops as well?"

Without thinking, I hand over the mugs' plastic screw-tops. "Have fun." The girls run off into the back yard, and I wonder idly what is growing out there in the middle of January that would fit in a travel mug. Mark appears beside me, and together we watch as the girls forage about in the far lush corners of the yard. I lean my head back into his chest and I assure both of us, "Look at them. Look how happy they are. This is going to be good, this move. Everything is going to work out."

After a few minutes, the girls come running back to the house. Kallan is having trouble screwing on the top of her travel mug, which confuses me for a moment, because I can think of no reason they needed the screw-tops in the first place, but then I watch as Kallan curls her body into the effort of tightening the top against obvious resistance, and realization dawns — whatever is in the travel mugs is struggling.

Maj holds her tightly sealed travel mug aloft. "The only reason Kallan is having trouble is she's got too many slugs. Mine fit perfectly."

Kallan gives up on getting her captives to cooperate, and she screws the top of her travel mug right through a slug's body; the severed half falls to the floor at our feet with a wet sticky sound, and the Labrador speed-undulates over to eat it. Kallan looks up at us. "What?"

"Slugs? That's what you were collecting? Slugs?"

Maj unscrews her travel mug and dumps her collection out onto the kitchen counter. The slugs emerge in one connected writhing mass, holding the cylindrical shape of their containment for a moment after release and then oozing urgently sideways and away.

Kallan dumps out her container as well, pounding her travel mug onto the counter several times, severing a few more freakishly large slug bodies in the process.

Mark has taken several steps back by now. "Well, this is horrifying."

I pick up the travel-mugs and peer into their slimy withins, a bit nauseated at the thought of ever using them for coffee again.

Kallan runs a hand over the slippery mass of oozing creatures, separating out a few dead chunks and tossing them to the eagerly undulating dog. She smiles. "OK, huge slugs are a giant point in Oregon's favor."

Maj grabs a handful of slugs and reaches to take a travel mug from my hand; she stuffs the slugs back into the container and addresses Kallan, "OK, listen up. I saw a shovel in the garage. Let's go dig a hole in the back yard for the slugs to live in."

Kallan scoops her slugs and crams them into the other travel mug. "Maj, you are a genius!"

"Maj?"

Maj pauses. "Yes, Mother?"

"Why do you need to sanitize after most contact with the world, but you are untroubled by slug-slime?"

"Don't be silly, Mother ... it's people who carry the germs that do you in, not slugs." She leans to coo into her travel mug, "Right, ugly snuggly slugly boys?"

Mark and I watch as the girls lug the shovel and the slugs out to a far corner of the yard. Kallan comes racing back across the yard to grab the hose, which she drags to the hole. "Maj, I'm pretty sure slugs love to swim! We'll dig a pool for them!"

"Look," I say weakly, "Look at how happy they are. Look at how much fun they are having slaughtering wildlife."

Mark hugs me. "This is going to be good, this move. Everything is going to work out."

Mating with snack food

We've landed in Lake Oswego, a small tree-lined community not so far from Portland. The city of Lake Oswego surrounds a small private lake called, strangely enough, Oswego Lake. The Willamette River is less than ten minutes away. There are parks and green spaces and trails everywhere. The schools are excellent. The neighbors seem friendly (almost suspiciously so), and children roam the streets on their bicycles and scooters, disappearing into one another's houses with nary a phone call alerting any parent to any child's whereabouts. Mark says it's like we've traveled back in time to the 1950s, which is true and odd and lovely and disconcerting, all at once.

It turns out to be almost a week before the moving van arrives with our belongings, which brings to an end one of Kallan's favorite things about our new neighborhood, which is the gullibility of its children. She has managed to convince several awestruck new friends that we are squatters. "We used to be homeless," she informs the neighborhood children casually as she gives them tours of our furniture-free 'stolen' home, "but then it occurred to us that there are empty houses just sitting there waiting for us to use them. My dad kicked in the door, and here we are."

The thought of Mark kicking down a door makes me laugh.

Those same children now line the street and watch as our furniture and endless boxes of belongings are delivered and placed throughout the house.

Kallan hurries out to inform them that the first story was merely a cover for the truth, which is that we are in the witness-protection program. "We're all dangerous criminals," she tells them, "but the government needed us as witnesses against even more dangerous criminals, and so lucky you ... you get to live with heinous murderers in your midst! Don't worry," she reassures them, "unless we get super-bored, it's not like we kill people for fun."

Maj stands with me in the driveway, listening to her sister. "Do you hear her, Mother? It was bad enough people thought we were squatters; now she's telling them we're hired assassins. She is a lunatic." She yells at Kallan, **"STOP TELLING THEM I AM A MURDERER OR I WILL KILL YOU,"** and then she watches as the children's eyes go wide with delight and terror. Maj turns to me. "I possibly could have handled that better."

"No one thinks you're a murderer, Maj."

"They do think we're insane, though." She turns to point at Jack the terrier. "And his back-yard outfit is not helping."

At the moment, Jack looks relatively normal, if a bit overdressed; he's wearing a plaid sweater, a collar and leash, and an additional collar that delivers a jolt of electricity every time he barks wildly, this last item an attempt to bring his ceaseless barking under control. He looks annoyed but not exactly insane, although I know what Maj is talking about. The back yard at this new house is enclosed with a tall wooden fence. It's a big yard, and Persie the Labrador loves it. Jack, however, took about three seconds to discover that while the fence is tall, it is not short; there are hundreds of possible ways for a small squirmy dog to leave the yard by going *under* the fence. I tried to block the larger gaps with rocks, but once he realized there was a way out, there was no stopping him.

This meant that every single time Jack wanted to go potty, I had to take him out on his leash, which grew very old very quickly once the rain started to fall. But as Jack has no loyalty whatsoever, and has spent his life seemingly convinced that we are holding him captive and keeping him from being reunited with his real family, letting him run free is not really an option. I tried tying Jack to a long tethered leash, but he managed to hog-tie himself almost immediately, and then he lay helpless and bound and screaming on the ground waiting for us to come get him.

And so I went to the pet-supply store and bought one of those plastic medical Elizabethan collars ... the kind they use to keep dogs from bothering a surgical site or some small injury. The only collar they had in Jack's size was bright purple, and so now, whenever he goes into the back yard, he wears a big plastic purple collar. Every time he comes upon a hole through which he used to be able to squirm, he bonks his coned-collar against the fence or the earth, and he turns away, thwarted. Jack doesn't mind the collar at all; he happily offers his head to be fitted before racing out into the yard, where he jumps and runs and plays with no hindrance or sense of embarrassment whatsoever.

Maj sighs. "Everybody thinks you're weird, Mother. There's no point in trying to pretend that making your dog wear a plastic purple collar to play in the back yard is something regular people do. Because it is so not."

"Wait, no one even knows me yet! We've only been here a week," I protest, "Everyone thinks I'm weird?"

She eyes me. "They're not wrong."

Kallan races up the driveway. "Mom, I forgot to tell you. Emergency! Delilah the turtle is being weird with Snack the goldfish."

"Maybe Delilah finally figured out that Snack is a food item."

"No, I don't think so. Delilah has been chasing Snack around the tank with her front arms stretched out as far as they can go. It's like she's trying to hug Snack as they swim, but there's something strange about the hugging. She has her turtle toe-claws out as far as they can go, like she wants to hug Snack right up into her body. Delilah is super determined. Her butt comes up into the hug almost like she's going to flip upside-down." Kallan pauses and then adds, "Snack is not amused, and he has scratches on his gold."

"Huh. That sounds like Delilah is a boy."

"What?"

"That sounds like your turtle is trying to mate with Snack."

Taken aback, Kallan insists, "Delilah is not a boy!"

"Pretty sure."

Kallan is horrified, and she screams up at her bedroom window from where we stand in the driveway, "WE DO NOT HAVE SEX WITH SNACK! ARE YOU LISTENING TO ME, DELILAH? KEEP YOUR CLAWS TO YOURSELF! YOU ARE A GIRL, AND YOU ARE NOT TO MATE THE SNACK FOOD."

The wide-eyed children at the end of the driveway could not possibly be more in love with Kallan.

Kallan leans past her sister to shake her fist up at her bedroom window. "DO NOT SEX THE SNACK!" She stomps into the house past the movers, yelling as she goes, "THIS IS NOT OK, DELILAH. EAT SNACK IF YOU LIKE, BUT DO NOT MATE HIM. WE DO NOT HAVE SEX WITH SNACK FOODS. THAT IS ABSOLUTELY NOT OK."

I pat Maj on the shoulder. "People may think I'm weird, but no way they think I'm the weirdest of the new neighbors."

Maj points. "Mother?"

"Yes?"

"Jack is mating your leg."

Of course he is.

No more safety

We spend the next few days unpacking, assembling furniture, and rearranging belongings to make this house feel like our home. It rains every day, and because we are not used to doing things in the rain, the girls and I stare glumly out the window and wait for it to stop. The girls aren't scheduled to start school for a few days yet, and, in these last few moments before their new lives start in earnest, it turns out we don't know what to do with ourselves. Mark has no such issues; he sets up his office and commences networking and job-hunting, leaving the girls to stare at me and then out the window at the rain and then at me again. When there finally comes a break in the rain, I throw the bicycles and a large towel into the minivan and I hustle the girls into the car. "We're going on a bike ride. Hurry up before the clouds change their minds."

A few minutes later, we are unloading our bicycles beneath clearing skies, and then we ride together down a small shaded path to what the map promises is a playground.

When we find it, the playground is abandoned, which is no surprise, both because of the rain and because everyone is in school. I grab the towel and wipe the puddles from the equipment — a set of swings, a bank of five see-saws, and an impressively tall slide, all circa 1974. Playgrounds look nothing like this in California, and the girls are momentarily taken aback; everything is hard and sharp and metal, like the playground equipment I remember from my own childhood. There is not a primary plastic color to be found.

I wipe down a picnic bench and take a seat.

Maj sees danger everywhere. Kallan runs off to play.

After just a few minutes, I call Maj over.

"Oh my god, Maj ... stop yelling at your sister! I have things under control. I do not need you to help me."

Her hands are on her hips, and she glares at me. "OK, but you *do* need help. You are not saying the things that I am saying, so someone has to step in and say those things. If you are not going to do your job, someone has to do it."

"Really, Maj?"

"Yes. You're welcome."

"Babe, come sit with me for a minute." I pat the bench next to me.

Maj walks over and sits. "OK, but do you see her? She is walking down the slide! She is not holding on! She is just standing straight and tall and walking down the slide! It is a huge dangerous slide and she is walking down it and you are saying nothing. That is so dangerous. She could be killed! But do you care? No, you just want to talk to me about yelling too much."

"Yes. You are yelling too much."

She swings her feet in angry frustration. "Yeah, because clearly this is the bigger emergency. And when Kallan is dead? And someone wants to know how that happened? You can explain all about how you had to lecture me about how I should not be safe."

"Geez, Maj. Take a breath. There is no one else at this park. It's just the three of us. No one cares if Kallan is walking on the slide. Let it go."

"This is not just about the rules, Mother. Although it is **COMPLETELY** against the rules to walk on a slide. **HOW DO YOU NOT KNOW THIS?**"

I hold up my cellphone. "Listen, if Kallan falls and breaks all of her arms and legs, I will call 911 and they will come and get her. And then maybe I will get a small lecture from a doctor about letting Kallan walk down a slide. But guess what?"

"What?"

"After Kallan's casts come off and we head out one fine future day to play at the park? I am so going to let her walk down a slide again if she wants to walk down a slide."

"So basically, you are saying that you want Kallan dead."

I take a moment before answering. "Yes, Maj. That is correct. Soon after Kallan was born, I realized what a tragic mistake I had made. So my evil plan is to let Kallan play all wildly dangerously at the playground until she is dead, and then it will be just the two of us again, babe." I wrap my arm around Maj and give her a big squeeze. "Just the two of us. Like it was always meant to be."

"You are not even funny, Mother."

"I should probably ask Kallan to take off her bicycle helmet."

"So not funny."

Kallan runs up, her eyes alight with anticipation. "Maj! Come do the see-saws with me!"

See-sawing does not go well, and then there is Kallan standing alone in the middle of the see-saw, trying to gauge how far she can walk in one direction before the balance shifts.

And Maj is at my side, beside herself with rage. **"I COULD HAVE BEEN KILLED!"**

"I get it, Maj. She should not have leaped from the see-saw while you were still in the air. However, the lucky thing? Is that you have legs."

"What?"

"You have legs. Legs you used to stop the death. And then you were just standing and crabby. Not dead at all."

"YOU NEVER CARE WHEN SHE TRIES TO KILL ME."

Maj sits beside me in sullen not-killed silence for the next twenty minutes or so as Kallan plays by herself and emerges from the experience also un-killed. When it's time to head out, we continue bicycling along the same path, which the map assures me goes in a big lazy circle back to approximately where we parked the car. Kallan is in the lead, Maj second, and I bring up the rear.

It turns out that the path is not exactly a circle, although it's close. The final stretch of our bike ride is the only portion of our route that is not a paved bike path, a ½-mile stretch down a quiet tree-lined street to the parking lot where we left the car. Maj is not at all pleased that I have plunged us into dangerous traffic, and she is determined to scream us to the safety of our minivan. Actually, since Maj is in the middle, she can only see her sister, so the screaming is directed at Kallan's butt.

"KALLAN, WATCH OUT FOR CARS PULLING OUT!"

"STAY TO THE RIGHT! KALLAN! KALLAN! STAY TO THE RIGHT!"

"YIELD!"

"YIELD!"

"OK, NEVER MIND ... THAT CAR WASN'T MOVING, SO IT'S OK YOU FAILED TO YIELD."

"IF YOU DON'T SPEED UP, I AM GOING TO PASS YOU!"

"DON'T GO SO FAR AHEAD! YOU WILL LOSE US!"

"STAY TO THE RIGHT!"

"ACK! KALLAN, WHAT ARE YOU DOING? YOU CAN'T JUST STOP LIKE THAT IN THE MIDDLE OF THE ROAD! ARE YOU KIDDING ME?"

I pull up behind the two girls, and they are both yelling at me ...

From Maj: "MOTHER, I COULD HAVE BEEN KILLED! DID YOU SEE WHAT SHE DID? I COULD HAVE BEEN KILLED!"

From Kallan: "Mom, tell her to stop yelling at me! I'm not a baby. I am eight years old and I know how to ride a bicycle. She is all crazy and screaming at me for nothing at all. I DO NOT HAVE TO YIELD TO PARKED CARS!"

I point to Kallan. "OK, you ... Kallan. If you need to stop, you need to get off to the side of the road, right? Your sister should not need to swerve to avoid you."

Kallan nods. "Right, sorry."

I point to Maj. "And you? You are driving me completely insane. You do not get to yell anymore. At all. If you yell at your sister all bossy again, I am going to knock on one of these doors and give someone a free bike. And then you will be walking. Do you understand me?"

"Geez, you don't have to be so crabby."

"Do you understand me?"

She rolls her eyes. "Yes, OK. No more safety. Got it."

We pedal the short remaining distance to the car. Maj narrates.

"WOW, RISKING DEATH WITH EVERY TURN OF THE PEDALS IS WAY MORE FUN THAN BEING SAFE!"

"TEN YEARS IS ALL I NEED. I'VE LIVED A FULL LIFE! BRING ON THE DOOM!"

"I HAVE THROWN CAUTION AND SANITY TO THE WIND AND I HAVE NEVER FELT MORE ALIVE!"

"THAT'S RIGHT, KALLAN ... DISREGARD THE TRAFFIC SIGNS! WE ARE FUGITIVES FROM SAFETY!"

"I WELCOME DANGER! I AM GIDDY, I TELL YOU! GIDDY!"

"BRING ON THE MAYHEM, THAT'S WHAT I ALWAYS SAY!"

We pile our bikes into the back of the minivan, and I pull Maj aside as Kallan picks wildflowers. "Maj, listen ... I know this is a lot ... the move and all the changes, but I promise you that your father and I have everything under control. You don't need to be quite so ...," I search for the word, "vigilant."

Maj is surprised. "What are you talking about, Mother? This is how I always am."

Which is true.

We climb into the car.

Maj checks her seatbelt to be sure it is snug. "That was fun! We should go bike riding every day."

There is only silence in response.

Maj reaches forward for the bottle of hand sanitizer. "What?"

Wild carcass of modesty

The next day, I take the girls to the local science museum.

"We see you, Mother." Maj pulls on her raincoat. "You can't stand that you don't get to be in charge of our learning anymore."

Kallan agrees. "It's so obvious ... you just want to get in a little extra home-schooling before we cast you aside in favor of real teachers."

"I for one refuse to learn anything today, just so you know," Maj informs me.

"Me neither," says Kallan. "In fact? I am going to go out of my way to be ignorant."

I grab the car keys. "You two are a joy, you know that? Pure joy. This is exactly what I imagined motherhood would be like."

"Expectations are a dangerous thing, Mother."

I hit the remote to unlock the minivan. "Tell me, Maj ... do you expect to arrive at the museum undamaged?"

"DID YOU JUST THREATEN ME WITH BODILY INJURY, WOMAN?"

"There are different kinds of damage, Maj. I'm just suggesting you should keep your expectations low."

"WHY MUST I ALWAYS LIVE MY LIFE IN FEAR?"

On the way to the museum, we pass a sign that says "Prevent Child Abuse" in giant black letters. Time passes. There is talking of the aimless sort. There is always talking ... especially in the car and especially from Kallan. Kallan likes a seat-belted and captive audience. When she finally takes a breath, she asks, "Mom, can you turn on the radio?"

"OH MY GOSH, MOTHER ... SHE NEVER STOPS. SHE NEVER STOPS. MAKE HER STOP."

Kallan ignores her sister. "Mom, can you?"

As I reach for the radio, Maj interjects, "Listen up, Kallan ... you can either have the radio on or you can sing. I will not stand for both and that is not up for negotiation. My brain cannot travel down the two musical roads at once, so choose a fork and stick to it."

"Hmm." Kallan, who is accustomed to her sister's arbitrary demands, considers. "I choose to stick the fork of singing. No radio, Mom. Maj wants to hear me sing."

"THAT IS NOT WHAT I SAID."

"And now, I am going to serenade my sweet sister Maj."

"I REFUSE TO LISTEN TO YOU OR ACKNOWLEDGE YOU IN ANY WAY."

After a few bars of humming tunelessly, Kallan starts to sing ... "She wakes up in the morning and her smile is upside down."

"THIS HAD BETTER NOT BE ABOUT ME BECAUSE I WILL POUND YOU. I AM NOT FROWNY!"

"All the sides of the bed are incorrect and so she always gets up wrong."

"STOP SINGING ABOUT ME AND STOP LOOKING AT

ME WITH LOVEY EYES. I WILL NOT STAND FOR THIS!"

"She's a girl who points a finger."

"MOTHER, SILENCE THE BEAST YOU BIRTHED!"

"She's a girl with grief to give."

"YOU WANT TO SEE GRIEF? I WILL GIVE YOU GRIEF."

"She's never wronnnnngggggg ... You can ask her and she'll tell you .... She's never wronnngggg ... PRONG PRONG PRONG PRONG PRONG."

"WAIT, WHAT THE HECK IS THE PRONGING PART ABOUT?"

Kallan sings her answer as the next line of the song. "That's the sound of her death."

"MOTHER, THE VILLAINY AND EVIL IS SPILLING ACROSS THE MINIVAN AND INVADING MY PERSONAL SPACE."

"PRONG PRONG PRONG ... Stick a fork in her."

"DID YOU JUST THREATEN ME WITH STABBING?"

Kallan finishes her song with a flourish. "PRONG ... The girl is done."

There is silence for a moment as Maj seethes, and Kallan leans forward. "Did you see what I did there, Mom? She told me to choose a fork, and so I chose the fork of singing and I sang a song about sticking a fork in her ... because she's done ... although, by the way, I do not even understand what that phrase means except stabbing and so Maj had to die."

"I SERIOUSLY CANNOT BELIEVE THAT YOU ALLOW HER TO SING AT ME THIS WAY, MOTHER." Maj turns to Kallan. "Also, by the way, the poky parts of a fork are called tines."

I correct her. "Actually, *prong* is a perfectly acceptable word for the poky parts of a fork."

Kallan yells "YAY!" and Maj says disgustedly, "Seriously, Mother?"

"Seriously, Maj."

"THIS FAMILY ANNOYS ME."

There is quiet for about three seconds, and then Kallan wonders aloud why Oregon is so concerned about fat kids.

I have no idea what she is talking about. "Ummmmm ... what?"

She explains, "Maybe because we were home-schooling for a while, we didn't get all the messages, but up here in Oregon, let me tell you, they are very worried about fat kids. Which is weird, because they tell us not to call names or be rude to people or point out how other people are different than we are because we will hurt their feelings. But whoever is in charge of worrying about fatness does not seem to be at all concerned about pointing out the fat or hurting fat kids' feelings. Those billboards are all over the place up here in Oregon."

I'm confused. "What are you talking about, Kallan? Who's worried about fat kids?"

Kallan is incredulous. "What do you mean *Who's worried about fat kids?* Those signs are all over the place. We pass them all the time."

"What signs?"

Cranky now that her mother is so clueless, Kallan reaches forward to wave her hands in irritated frustration. "Huge big signs on the side of the road. PREVENT CHILD ABUSE."

Maj lets loose a huge sarcastic **"HAHAHAHA!!!!"** and then a nasty, **"YOU ARE SO DUMB. I CAN'T BELIEVE HOW DUMB YOU ARE."**

I glance up in the handy minivan interior mirror to see Kallan balling up a fist as she announces, "Somebody better make Maj stop or I am going to pound her."

"Apologize to your sister, Maj."

Maj apologizes, "Sorry you don't even know how to read a billboard, dear sister."

I reach a hand back to swipe angrily at Maj. "That is exactly the sort of apology that gets you pounded, Maj."

Kallan still has her fist optimistically poised in the air, ready to pound if I grant permission. I reach back to wave her clenched hand into her lap as I explain, "*Obese* means fat, Kallan. The word on the billboards is *abuse*, which means when someone hurts you. The signs are saying that moms and dads need to be careful with their emotions and their tempers and not hurt their children."

Silence in the car for a minute and then another question from Kallan. "OK, but then why would they use a word that means all of the fat kids are stupid?"

That one takes me a minute. "No, baby ... that's another word. Are you thinking of **obtuse**?"

Kallan murmurs sulkily, "Oh yeah."

Maj, in nasty triumph, crows, "HAHAHA!!! That is the most obtusey-est thing I have ever heard!"

My arm swings back again to vertically cut the air between them. "Come on, ladies ... Maj, quit being a pain in the butt. Kallan, do not pound your sister."

Maj sticks her tongue out at Kallan. "Yeah, don't obese me."

Kallan reaches a hand across the minivan, her fingers rigid and extended. "Look, Maj ... I can turn my fingers into prongs."

"MOTHER, SHE IS MENACING ME WITH FINGERS OF PRONG-DOOM!"

There's the whiff of closely averted violence in the air now, but it's nothing a little music won't fix. "Time for the radio!" I punch buttons until I find a song. Something bouncy and cheerful, and, as it turns out, crazily inappropriate.

Kallan listens for a moment and then leans forward to ask, "In this song, why does she bring her junk to the party and once it's there, why does she care if the boys touch it? Even if they are drunk, it's not like you can really ruin junk."

"Ummmmm ..." I hesitate, but then offer, "I think *junk* in this song actually means her butt."

"SERIOUSLY???"

I answer over Maj's hysterical laughter. "Yup."

Kallan reaches her hand into her sister's space again. "You hush up, or I will prong your junk."

"THAT IS SO INAPPROPRIATE. YOU ARE LIKE A WILD CARCASS OF MODESTY! ROAD-KILL MODESTY! MY SISTER IS ROAD-KILL MODESTY!"

"What does that even mean, Maj?" Kallan is not unflattered, but she is confused.

"NOT EVERYTHING HAS TO MAKE SENSE. SOMETIMES EMOTIONS WRANGLE THE WORDS!"

Kallan considers. "Well, it's never boring with you, Maj. I'll give you that."

**"DITTO, AND THAT IS NOT A COMPLIMENT, SO DON'T
YOU DARE TAKE IT AS A COMPLIMENT."**

"Too late."

.....

The Oregon Museum of Science and Industry turns out to
be a fantastic museum, although within minutes of entering,
Kallan is standing next to life-sized images of a naked man and
woman (part of a display on reproductive health) asking, "OK,
Mom? When are you going to get to the part where you tell me
how all of this goes together to make a baby?"

I try distraction. "Hey! I think they have one of those machines
where you crank the handle and smash a cool picture onto a
penny!"

"Seriously, Mom?" Kallan turns to the photos. "How about if I
point to the areas I think are involved, and you tell me if I'm
getting warm?"

Maj saves me, but inadvertently. She waves at Kallan from the
room across the hall. **"KALLAN, THEY HAVE THE
BIGGEST FROGS I'VE EVER SEEN! AND TURTLES,
TOO! COME ON!"**

A bit later, we discover a chemistry lab in which the lab assistant
insists we all put on protective goggles. I try a couple of different
pairs, but I must have a weirdly shaped skull or something,
because they all seem to fit too tightly across my face. Maj and
Kallan are dancing with impatience, so I finally just grab a
random green pair and figure, *How bad could it be?*

As I watch Maj and Kallan excitedly running experiments, I
realize the girls were right when they accused me of trying to
squeeze in a bit of education before they start at their new school;
I'm going to miss home-schooling them. As amazing as their new
school is going to be, a part of me mourns the change. As the girls
mix chemicals and light Bunsen burners, I toss in a few words of
scientific advice here, a helpful definition or concept there, but I
stop when I see the girls glance at one another and, in perfect

sister-unison, roll their eyes behind their goggles.

We linger in the chemistry lab for perhaps 45 minutes, long enough that I stop being aware of the discomfort of the ill-fitting goggles. When I remove the goggles and run my fingers over my face, I feel an impossibly deep groove across my forehead. The bathroom mirror confirms the extent of my temporary deformity; I look as though I have recently had some sort of experimental back-alley brain surgery.

I try to pull my hair into messy camouflaging bangs, but the girls keep sweeping my hair back to loudly check on my "brain scar."

"Is this what happens when you get old, Mother?" Maj asks pityingly, "Your flesh just holds the mold of whatever has most recently damaged you?"

I am annoyed and self-conscious. "Yes, Maj ... want to see the imprint of your birth?"

She runs away screaming in horror, which is deeply satisfying. She doesn't run far, though, because although Maj loves museums, she is sometimes overwhelmed by her aversion to the closeness of other people and their messiness. Everywhere she turns, there are children — either too young for school or here in rowdy field-trip groups — and none of them seem inclined to respect her demands for personal space and hygiene. Kallan disappears into a room filled with vacuum hoses and air tunnels, a room in which one can fashion machines that shoot out or suck up little blue rubber balls; there is no way Maj is entering that room. She spends her time instead alone, watching an intricate demonstration of the normal bell-curve while her sister cavorts with the other screaming, tube-assembling, vacuum-sucking, ball-hurling children.

I am accustomed to Maj's issues with germs. The room of shrieking snotty children is a little off-putting to me as well. I don't mind that Maj carries hand sanitizer around with her, or that she pulls her sleeves over her hands to open doors, or that she ducks away with horrified eyes from a nearby child who suddenly sneezes or coughs. I have even grown accustomed to her weird sideways hugs and kisses, designed to minimize germ exchange.

But at the moment, my forehead still dented and my bangs still ridiculous, my ego still bruised ... I am not in the mood.

Maj returns; she already knows the answer to the question she is about to ask, but she asks it anyway. "Mother, what did you pack us for lunch?"

"I packed us money to buy food in the cafeteria."

"Mother, it's like when you leave the house in the morning, you forget exactly who you are parenting. I am Maj, and eating food in cafeterias is troublesome for me. You are supposed to pack me food."

"Come on, Maj ... let me get your sister, and we'll go have lunch; the cafeteria will be an adventure."

After much discussion, Kallan orders a slice of pizza and Maj agrees to nothing at all. Frustrated, I order a salad/sandwich combo to split with her. I carefully sanitize my hands before touching anything, and then I cut the sandwich in half. "Here, Maj ... you can have the bigger half." I push the bigger half of the sandwich to her side of the large plate we are sharing.

"Mother, now that you have shoved my portion of the sandwich, everything within the sandwich-half has been thrown slightly off-kilter."

I put down my half of the sandwich, from which I was just about to take a bite. "What's your point, Maj?"

She picks up her fork and stabs at her half of the sandwich angrily. "My half of the sandwich has not maintained its sandwich-integrity. Look at it," she says as she stabs at it a few more vicious times, "it's falling apart."

I watch as her sandwich-half disintegrates under the assault. "Seems unlikely you are going to be able to stab your way to a solution."

She throws her fork down. "Look at it, Mother. I trusted you to split the sandwich fairly, but my half is all garbaged."

I hold out my half of the sandwich, from which I have still not taken a bite. "You want to trade? It's fine with me if you want to trade."

"MOTHER, YOU'VE HELD THAT SANDWICH HALF WITH YOUR CLAW HANDS INTENDING TO EAT IT ... HOW COULD YOU OFFER ME A SANDWICH THAT IS SLOBBERED WITH INTENTION AND SQUEEZED IN CLAW-GRIP?"

Kallan pauses mid-bite, the melty cheese of her pizza draping from her mouth as she speaks. "You want some of my pizza, Maj?"

Maj turns to her sister with surprising calmness. "If you knew how close my brain comes to exploding right out of my skull when you say things like that, you would be more cautious with your words."

Kallan sticks her tongue out to loop a stray strand of cheese into her mouth. "If you get brains on this pizza, I'm going to pee more than my initials on your floor."

"WHAT ARE YOU SAYING? YOU WILL PEE A MANIFESTO OF HATRED INTO MY PILLOW? IS THAT WHAT YOU ARE SAYING?"

Kallan wrestles her pizza into submission. "As soon as I figure out what a manifesto is, I am so peeing it on your pillow. So keep your brains to yourself."

"I DO NOT HAVE TO KEEP MY BRAINS TO MYSELF! I WILL NOT HAVE MY INTELLIGENCE CAGED!"

"Maj, I was talking about the brain explosion you threatened ... go ahead and be as smart as you want."

"Oh. That's different." Maj returns her attention to me and the half-sandwich that remains. "Seriously, Mother? I look away for an instant, and you ate the better half of the sandwich?"

"I offered it to you. I said I would trade."

"You know better than to act on my first rejection, Mother."

"Whatever. I was hungry. Are you going to eat the stabbed half?"

"Obviously not, Mother." But before I can reach to eat that half of the sandwich as well, she garbles it up in a napkin and stands to throw it in the nearby garbage can.

Leaving us the salad, which is arranged on the same large plate that held the sandwich. After the fiasco of the sandwich splitting, I am not inclined to try to separate lettuce leaves and bits of crouton into equal shares, and so I lean forward to stab delicately at a cherry tomato as I say, "I will be very careful to only touch my fork to the items I eat, OK?"

Maj sinks back in her chair and stares at me incredulously as I chew the single tomato. "Well, thank you very much. It's not enough I didn't get to eat any of the sandwich; now I don't get to eat any salad either."

"Maj, I only touched the single tomato, and then I ate that exact tomato. I touched nothing else."

"MOTHER, LET ME BE PERFECTLY CLEAR ... I CANNOT EAT ANY PART OF THIS SALAD NOW THAT YOU HAVE PUT YOUR SPIT ALL OVER IT."

Kallan whispers through her cheese looping, "Prong, prong, prong."

I glance around at the many tables of happily lunching people, all of whom are staring in our direction thanks to Maj's outburst. Without saying a word, I reach with my fork to enthusiastically rummage through the salad looking for another tomato.

"MOTHERS ARE NOT SUPPOSED TO GREED-SLOBBER THEIR CHILDREN'S FOOD, MOTHER!"

More whispering from Kallan ... "Prongity prong prong prong."

I seriously contemplate leaning forward to drool into the plate.

Kallan works to control the cheese of her pizza. "Mom, you should have another baby."

I take a big bite of salad. "That is so not going to happen."

"Awww ... it would be awesome. I would finally have the sister I always wanted."

Maj turns to tap on Kallan's shoulder. "Hello? It's me. The sister you always wanted who was here before you arrived."

Kallan takes another messy bite of pizza. "Yeah, except turns out you're not the sister I've always wanted. The sister I've always wanted is named Beatrice, and she's nice to me."

"I'M NICE TO YOU, YOUNG LADY. I AM AS NICE AS ANYONE IN MY POSITION COULD EVER DREAM OF BEING." Maj leans back in her chair to angrily watch me eat the salad. "Anyway, Mother's too old to have more babies."

I sigh and then smile at Maj, my hand to my heart. "These are the kinds of moments that make being your mother worthwhile, Maj."

"Sorry, Mother ... newsflash ... you are old."

"Like I said, Maj ... you make my heart swell with gratitude for the gifts motherhood has given me."

Maj points at me. "That right there? Old-lady sarcasm."

I turn to Kallan. "No more babies. It's just you and your sister for as far as the eye can see."

Kallan shrugs. "That's alright. Maybe I can start wearing a blindfold."

"WHAT DID SHE JUST SAY? I BELIEVE SHE IS USING THE NOTION OF BEING HANDICAPPED TO SULLY MY SISTERLY EXISTENCE. SLAM HER TO THE GROUND, MOTHER. SLAP HER WHILE SHE'S BLIND!"

I lean across the table to whisper to Kallan, "You are the sister I always dreamed Maj would have."

Kallan giggles, and Maj demands to know, **"WHY ARE EVERYONE'S DREAMS COMING TRUE BUT MINE?"**

"Salad?" I extend a forkful of salad in Maj's direction as though she might take a bite from my fork.

She glares at me and then stands. "If you need me, I'll be over there horror-barfing by the demonstration of the normal bell-curve."

I call after her, "Stand to one side, Maj. Far to one side."

Kallan watches her sister stalk away. "Good one, Mom."

In the end, Maj eats nothing, and after a few more exhibits, it's time to drive home.

"I AM WRETCHEDLY HUNGRY, MOTHER ... SO IF YOU WERE THINKING OF RATING YOUR PARENTING FOR THE DAY, THINK IN TERMS OF NEGATIVITY."

I swing the car out of the parking lot. "I always do, Maj."

"YES, INDEED. IF I HAD A BROWN PAPER BAG ... LIKE SAY THE SORT A BETTER MOTHER MIGHT HAVE THOUGHT TO PACK A LUNCH IN ... I WOULD FILL IT WITH THE LUMPS OF YOUR FAILURE-RIDDEN DAY."

"And I would take that brown paper bag and top it off with poo and light it afire outside your bedroom, and then you would come running to stomp out the flames and you would be covered in dog-poo and failure lumps and also possibly you would be a little singed around the ankles and calves."

Kallan bursts into hysterical laughter. "Oh my gosh, Mom, I was so thinking you meant you would put your own poo in the bag, and then you said dog-poo, which makes more sense and that is the funniest thing I have ever heard!"

Maj stares out the window angrily. "This family is not the family I deserve."

"Mom, can you put on the radio?" Kallan bounces in her seat. "Please?"

"MOTHER, DON'T YOU DARE PUT ON THE RADIO. I HAVE HAD IT WITH THIS FAMILY AND HAPPY RHYTHMIC NOISES."

As I consider, Maj says, "Mother, in case you were wondering, you still have a forehead dent of old-lady playdough skin."

So I decide, "Kallan gets to choose ... radio or singing."

Kallan yells out joyfully, "I CHOOSE SINGING!" She clears her throat and sings the song she made up earlier:

She wakes up in the morning and her smile is upside down
all the sides of the bed are incorrect
and so she always gets up wrong
she's a girl who points a finger
she's a girl with grief to give

She's never wronnnnnggggggg ...
you can ask her and she'll tell you ....
she's never wronnngggg ...

PRONG PRONG PRONG PRONG PRONG.

That's the sound of her death
PRONG PRONG PRONG ...
stick a fork in her

PRONG ...

the girl is done

Uncharacteristically silent during the singing, Maj now announces, "**MOTHER ... I AM SO DONE. I AM DONE WITH ALL OF THIS. I AM DONE.**"

Kallan is delighted that Maj has inadvertently taken up the song, and she goes operatic and top-volume for the last refrain ...

PRONG ...
Stick a fork in her ...
The girl is done.

"**AIIAIEIEIEEIEEEEEEEEEE!**"

Serving from the toilet

The day before the girls start at their new school, we decide to make spaghetti and invite some just-met possible friends to join us for dinner. All four of us are tired of talking about what school will be like; we need a distraction. The couple we invited is also new to the area, and they have two small children, much younger than our daughters ... it should be a simple and stress-free evening.

With a half hour to go before our guests are due to arrive, Mark puts the water on the stovetop to boil and I search the basement pantry for noodles. For some reason, the girls have strong and differing opinions about the diameter of the noodles to be boiled. They voice these opinions stridently enough that Mark walks downstairs with opinions of his own, and soon the four of us are arguing the relative merits of spaghetti versus capellini. Finally, I can't stand it anymore, and I *eenie-meenie-miney-mo* between the two packages of pasta. I hold up the winner. "Capellini it is!"

For some reason, this pleases no one, and so, thinking perhaps we have all been arguing for the same thing without realizing it, I say, "Or we could have the spaghetti ..."

And then everyone is arguing again.

Somehow, after more bickering, we finally settle on spaghetti noodles. Before Mark joined us downstairs to debate pasta, he threw Jack the terrier a yellow rubber bone to keep him occupied and off the dining-room table. Jack has been known to climb up onto the table to see what is being served, and while that is sometimes funny, the dining room's large windows in this house look out on the front porch. A small disheveled dog standing in the middle of the table helping himself to bread and sipping milk from a glass is not the first impression we hope to make on our guests.

So Jack followed us downstairs, bone in his mouth, to listen to the noodle fracas; he remains downstairs happily chewing on the rubber bone as the four of us walk upstairs to discover ... that the main floor of the house is filled with gas.

Mark had turned the gas on under the pasta water, but he failed to notice that it hadn't actually ignited. With twenty minutes to go before our guests arrive, the girls and I open every window and door and try to clear the poisonous gas from the house. I run around waving my hands and yelling, "No one light a match! No one make a spark!" while Mark fiddles with the stovetop knobs and ignites the flame beneath the pot of water. I pause in my hysteria. "Really, Mark?"

"You guys carry on with the pretend emergency," he says, and he proceeds with the serious business of pouring sauce from a jar into a pan. The girls and I walk around the house flapping magazines in the air, trying to disperse the toxicity, and we eventually end up surrounding Mark, who is stirring the sauce. We flap our magazines weakly, and he turns to look at us. "What?"

Maj and Kallan stand on either side of me, and we all three glare at him as I say, "I just want to be clear. Your thinking goes something like ... *Yes, we might all be killed in a giant gaseous explosion, and yes, that would be bad, but on the off chance that doesn't happen, I'm going to be sure to get this sauce warmed up.*"

Mark shrugs. "It smells a little bit, but once there's a flame safely ignited, the chances of a house-destroying fireball diminish somewhat."

"Did you seriously just try to reassure us and then also use the phrase *house-destroying fireball*?"

Instead of responding, Mark starts barking out orders. "Someone bring me a cistern!"

None of the three of us move; the girls don't know what a cistern is, so they are confused about how to proceed. I do know what a cistern is, and I am equally uncertain about the next step Mark envisions. "Umm, babe? Why exactly do you need a cistern?"

"Oh for god's sake, must everything in this family be a debate?" Mark is impatient, and he flails a sauce-covered spoon in the air as he issues his demand again. "I need a cistern! Why can't anybody just do what I ask without asking so many questions?"

"OK, but you need the cistern for ..."

"What is wrong with you, Kris? I need to pour the sauce into a cistern for serving. Why isn't someone moving? Get me a cistern!"

Kallan runs off as though she means to fetch a cistern, and I explain to Mark as Maj giggles, "Thing is, though ... a cistern is a huge cement receptacle in which one might, for example, store rainwater." I pretend to ponder his request more fully. "Unless you meant you want the cistern from the back of the toilet?"

Mark's irritation fades as it occurs to him he may have misspoken. "What?"

I continue, overly thoughtful, "Because the tank that holds the water for flushing is a cistern ... were you planning on serving the spaghetti sauce from the toilet? I'm totally on board, if that's your plan ... how exciting! I just want to be sure we're on the same page."

Before Mark can answer, there is screaming from downstairs ... Kallan's voice ... something about blood.

Mark and Maj and I all walk downstairs to greet a still-screaming Kallan, who is standing in the midst of gory nightmare. Somehow, Jack has cut his mouth on the soft rubber bone. Another dog might wisely have decided that once blood has been drawn, that is probably enough play with that particular toy. But Jack is a terrier, and he seems to have interpreted the blood (even though the blood is his own) as an escalation in the battle between dog and bone. So he has gone nuts, grabbing the bone by its rubber jugular and trying to shake the life out of it.

Streams of bloody drool have been sprayed and thrown all over a large area of wall and carpet at the bottom of the basement stairs.

Kallan stops screaming long enough to point out, "Look at him. He looks like he's been ripping the heads off squirrels."

With ten minutes to go before our guests are due to arrive, I am chasing a bloody-faced terrier around the house, trying to convince him to give up his bone. I eventually catch him and lock him in the basement shower, where he immediately begins to bark unstoppingly.

BARK BARK BARK BARK BARK BARK

"Shut up, Jack!" I turn to the girls. "Where is his shock collar?"

Maj goes in search of the shock collar while Kallan stays behind to help me wipe up the worst of the spattered gore from our walls and carpet.

BARK BARK BARK BARK BARK BARK

Maj reappears with the collar. "Want me to put it on Jack?"

"You think?"

"No need to be sarcastic, Mother."

BARK BARK BARK BARK BARK BARK

Kallan looks at me helplessly. "We're going to need carpet-cleaner ... it's not coming up." She considers. "This is why in Medieval times, they had stone floors with drains so the blood of torture and death could be easily rinsed away."

BARK BARK BARK BARK BARK BARK BARK

I answer Kallan, "Just do the best you can; we'll try to keep our guests out of the basement."

BARK BARK BARK BARK BARK BARK

Maj reappears, shock collar still in her hand. "I'm not touching him."

I am on my hands and knees, mopping up bloody drool, and I turn to glare at Maj. "Maj, I know his face is bloody, but I need you to put his shock collar on ... he is driving me insane with his barking."

BARK BARK BARK BARK BARK BARK

Maj shakes her head. "He poo-ed in the shower."

"He did what?"

BARK BARK BARK BARK BARK BARK

Kallan is thrilled. She runs off to check and is almost immediately back with a report. "Mom, there is poo everywhere. He is dancing in it. It's EVERYWHERE."

Maj stands with her arms crossed tightly across her chest. "I told you so. I'm not touching him."

BARK BARK BARK BARK BARK BARK BARK

I swipe at a bloody smear along the wall. "Our guests are going to be here any minute."

BARK BARK BARK BARK BARK BARK BARK BARK

The girls await instructions. I sigh. "OK, Maj? You go get me a change of clothes ... everything I am wearing is stained with drool and blood. And Kallan? You go get me a few towels and a bottle of shampoo."

Kallan is incredulous. "You're going to take a shower with him?"

"Maybe I'm going to kill him and pour every ounce of his terrier blood down the drain ... I haven't decided yet."

BARK BARK BARK BARK BARK BARK

The girls return with the items I requested, and I send them back upstairs with instructions. "When our guests get here, tell them I lost track of time, and that I'll be out of the shower in a minute. Try not to say anything about ...," I spread my arms sadly to encompass the gas and the blood and the drool and the toilet-served meal and the shower filled with dog poo and the entirety of the evening's preparations, " ... any of this."

Kallan nods, and Maj nods as well. "Lying by omission ... got it."

BARK BARK BARK BARK BARK BARK BARK

Resignedly, I walk to the bathroom and open the shower door. Jack stares up at me, bloody-muzzled, his tail wagging excitedly. He is covered in poo. He has hopped and pranced in the poo and tappity-danced little footprints of poo over every square inch of the shower's tiled floor. "Really, dog? Really?" I unroll huge lengths of toilet paper and wipe frantically at the floor, throwing each handful of mess into the toilet and flushing ... again ... and again ... and again ...

I reach to turn the shower on ... cold water, because hot will overwhelm me with the steamy warmed scent of defecation.

BARK BARK BARK BARK BARK BARK BARK

I step into the shower with him and close the door. As the water hits him, the remaining poo and blood are rinsed away ... and I am left standing in a soupy horror. Quickly, I lather him up with shampoo and rinse him off. Just as quickly, I lather myself up and rinse off, pausing to nudge a few larger pieces of poo toward the drain with my foot. "Why do I love you, Jack? No other dog in the world behaves this way."

BARK BARK BARK BARK BARK BARK

"Oh my god ... shut up." I turn off the shower and wrap him in a towel. I dry myself off, get dressed in the clean clothes Maj brought me, and then rub Jack dry. I hug his newly adorable teddy-bear dogness to my chest and I whisper in his ear, "OK, we're going to go upstairs and meet our guests. Try to make a good impression." He licks my cheek in seeming agreement.

Mark meets me at the top of the stairs. "Everything under control?"

"What's that chemical they use at crime scenes to check for traces of blood and bodily fluids?"

He thinks for a moment. "Luminol."

"Yeah, so let's just say that if, when we eventually move out of this house, Luminal is involved in the landlord's move-out inspection, we are going to have some explaining to do."

He laughs. "They're not here yet, by the way. Running late, I suppose." He hugs me. "So take a few minutes to relax."

At this exact moment, there is an ominous beeping from the laundry room off of the kitchen, where the washing machine is flashing and squalling excitedly about **"F-11, F-11, F-11!!!!"**

Mark consults the owner's manual, which came with the rental papers. "Apparently, F-11 is a failure of some sort."

I sigh. "Of course it is."

Mark and I begin stabbing at buttons trying to make the beeping stop. Kallan squeezes into the laundry room with us, and over the sound of our frustration and the ceaseless beeping, she says,

"Something's going wrong with Delilah's tank filter. I need one of you guys to come upstairs and help me clean it out and figure out what's going wrong."

Persie skulks into the laundry room with us, using her legs but just barely; she is as low to the ground as she can possibly be, and she soldier-crawls to the apparent safety of the tiny bathroom just beyond the laundry room.

Jack decides he should probably alert us to the possible emergency the beeping indicates .... BARK BARK BARK BARK BARK BARK

And then Maj is there as well, yelling over all of the other noise as though everything going on in this moment cannot possibly be as important as her demand that I go to the store the next day while she is at school and buy her knee-socks to go with her new boots.

And then the phone rings.

I wave for the girls to stop talking. Mark grabs Jack and snaps his shock collar into place. I walk away from the still-beeping washing machine and I answer the phone. "Hello?"

It's our would-be guests. Canceling from their car. They are apologetic ... there is an accident on the road ahead of where they are sitting; traffic is bad and they aren't even halfway to our house and their kids are screaming and impatient and hungry and it's just more than they can do. I can hear the screaming in the background as the parents apologize again. They're going to turn around and go home. Too much chaos, they tell me.

I hang up the phone and explain the cancellation to Mark and the girls, and then I laugh.

Mark and the girls start laughing as well, and we can't stop; several helpless minutes of hysteria pass against the beep of the washing machine's failure messages.

When we finally regain a small amount of control, I wipe my eyes and apologize, "I'm so sorry, girls ... this is not how your father and I meant for this evening to go."

Maj giggles. "Are you kidding me, Mother? This is the best evening we have had in this house so far."

Kallan agrees, "Seriously ... this house finally feels a little bit like home."

Mark unplugs the washing machine and summons us to the dinner table. He places a serving bowl filled with spaghetti and sauce on the table. Once everyone has been served food, Mark raises his glass in a toast. "Here's to new beginnings and chaos and laughter and love." Without lowering his glass, he adds, "Oh, and the word I was looking for earlier ... I meant *tureen*, not *cistern*."

I hesitate, but just for an instant. "Of course, you realize that *tureen* is incorrect as well."

He turns to me. "You are sometimes a little bit annoying."

The girls nod happy agreement, their mouths full of spaghetti, but not so full they can't give voice to the consensus.

"She so is."

"You so are, Mother."

Whatever.

Everything changes

The school bus arrives and takes the girls away.

I spend the day staring out the window, waiting for the school bus to bring them back to me.

"This is a good thing, Kris. This is why we moved here."

"I know."

Still.

She's not you

A week goes by, and then another. Despite the fact that she enjoyed home-schooling, fifth-grader Maj greets her return to "regular school" as though she has been finally thrown a life preserver after a long exhausting period of treading water. It's difficult not to feel a tiny betrayed by her happiness, even as I am thrilled that things are going so well for her.

Maj's single frustration is the fact that everyone here wants to call her Madge or Marge. "Kallan's name is easy ... even if someone messes it up, it's simple to explain it sounds like the first two syllables of the word *calendar*. I have to go around telling people my name sounds like the *Taj* in *Taj Mahal*, but guess what, Mother? No one knows what the Taj Mahal is, and so I've been getting a lot of blank stares."

I try to solicit more details about Maj's time at school, but after several days of side-stepping my inquiries, she says, "Mother, the thing is ... you've been a part of every single second of my life for the last 18 months." She looks at me a little sheepishly. "Is it OK if I don't share school with you, at least for a while? I like having something that's just mine. It's going well, Mother ... really well."

I nod. "That makes sense. You'll let me know if you need anything?"

"Obviously, Mother." Maj smiles. "Thank you."

Third-grader Kallan, on the other hand, is having more difficulty.

She misses spending her days with Maj and me. She is having difficulty adjusting to the classroom setting. Kallan takes me aside, her face serious. "What if it turns out I don't want to do regular school?"

"Why don't we back up a few steps ... what seems to be the problem?"

It turns out Kallan has a list, and she ticks off her points one at a time. "First thing? My teacher has rules for everything, and I do not like to have so many rules. I have informed her that I do better with fewer rules, and guess what? She doesn't care. She actually said that, right to my face ... *I — don't — care.*"

I stifle giggles at Kallan's incredulity. "She has a lot of students to teach. She probably needs rules to keep everything organized and on track."

Kallan rolls her eyes. "There are folders on her desk ... endless folders ... all different colors, and each folder is for a specific thing, and if you put your papers in the wrong folder, she acts like you never turned them in even though she obviously saw them when she opened the folder that turned out to be the wrong folder for those particular papers."

"You'll get used to how things work."

"Plus, she gives out points for good behavior, and you can trade your points for prizes, and guess what the main prize is that everyone is trying to earn?"

"What's that?"

"If I earn enough points, I'm allowed to eat lunch with one of the older kids during their lunch period. The only older kid I know well enough to eat lunch with is Maj, and Maj would kill me if I showed up at her lunch period all happy and sisterly."

"She would indeed."

Kallan shrugs her shoulders. "So I'm not as motivated toward good behavior as I might be if the prize was something other than being murdered by my sister."

"Yes, I can understand that. Although you might consider being well behaved just for the sake of being well behaved."

She rolls her eyes again. "Right."

"Is there anything else? Something I might actually be able to help with?"

Kallan looks at me sadly. "I'm not used to having to sit quietly for so long, and let me tell you ... my teacher does not enjoy being interrupted."

This time I don't bother stifling my laughter. "What did she say, exactly?"

Kallan does her best impression of her teacher, which comes out as a military version of her sister. **"CLASS, I AM SAYING THIS FOR THE BENEFIT OF THE NEW STUDENT BUT ALL OF YOU COULD USE A REMINDER ... IF I AM TALKING AND YOU CAN HEAR ME TALKING IT IS NOT YOUR TURN TO TALK. RAISE YOUR HAND IF YOU HAVE SOMETHING TO OFFER, AND IF THERE COMES A MOMENT IN WHICH I BELIEVE YOU MIGHT BE ABLE TO MAKE A VALUABLE CONTRIBUTION TO THE CONVERSATION, I WILL CALL ON YOU."**

"Is that seriously how loudly she talks in the classroom?"

"It seriously is ... she tells us to use our inside voices, but her inside voice is definitely an outside voice."

"So then what is her outside voice like?"

Kallan smiles. "Her outside voice is a screaming-across-the-playground-bring-all-fun-to-a-halt-through-bellowed-menace voice."

"I do like how you describe things."

"That's another thing ... she told us the class was going to do *Show and Tell*, which I know is babyish, but I was looking forward to it anyway, except it's been over a week since she said that, and nothing has been getting shown or told and these rocks are getting heavy."

"Rocks?"

Kallan heaves her backpack up onto the table. "Yeah, I was going to tell the class about the rocks we studied last semester during home-schooling." She digs into her backpack and comes up with about fifteen pounds of geodes and crystals and small boulders, which she arranges in front of me. "See? I want to show these to the class, but she never sets aside time."

"Did you tell her you'd brought something to show the class?"

Kallan looks at me curiously. "Was I supposed to? I assumed there would be a set time for *Show and Tell*."

"Want me to write her a short email?"

"That would be good ... I'm tired of hauling these back and forth to school every day." She sighs. "So we're really not going to go back to home-schooling?"

"No, babe. Everything is going to work out, though. You'll see. There's going to be a period of adjustment. Home-schooling was an entirely different sort of experience, and so it makes sense that you'd have some difficulty stepping back into a regular classroom."

She starts repacking the rocks into her backpack. "So basically, you're not going to do anything?"

"Sweetie, I've done what there is to do. You and I met with your teacher before school started. She's a bit bossy, but she's a very nice woman. She has your best interests at heart, and from all reports, she is a very good teacher. The next part is your responsibility. This is a big change, and I know it's hard."

"Hmmph."

"You are crazily smart. Insanely smart. You're going to be fine."

"What if I'm not fine?"

"If you were having a serious problem, I would be there in a heartbeat, but what you're describing is just the frustration that comes with new situations and new people. I know your teacher frightens you, but she's very nice, and you're going to be fine. You just have to give her a chance; you have to get used to her."

Kallan pouts. "She's not you."

"I know that, baby ... but it's going to be alright. I promise."

"Fine." Kallan gathers her composure and then lifts her chin defiantly. "The thing is, though? I don't think my teacher appreciates me."

I pull Kallan into a hug. "No one appreciates you like I do, baby girl."

She heaves her backpack onto her shoulder and meets my eyes. "But if there was a real problem, you would help me?"

"Of course."

So, of course, because Kallan is a few steps ahead of me, over the days that follow, Kallan reports real problems ... every day, she comes home with dramatic and detailed stories of things that have gone wrong.

"Mom, she took away my cellphone for no reason, and I got scared, because you and Daddy gave me the phone so I could always reach you or Maj if there was an emergency, and I felt all alone and she wouldn't give it back."

I email the teacher to ask for more information, and she responds immediately, explaining that it is her policy to confiscate phones that repeatedly ring or play music during class, and that Kallan got the phone back at the end of the day.

"Hey, Kallan?" I look up from my computer and the email response. "Was your phone playing loud music during class?"

She looks up from her phone, which she neglected to mention had been returned to her. "What does that have to do with anything?"

The next day, Kallan arrives home weepy about having been kept in from recess to do punishment math problems. "She told me I couldn't go outside to play until I finished all the problems, and it took me the whole time, and so I got no recess," she wails.

I email the teacher to ask for more information, and she responds immediately, explaining that she kept Kallan in for a single recess to test her knowledge of the multiplication tables, because she wanted to know if Kallan was on pace with the rest of the class. She further informs me that Kallan enthusiastically stayed inside and skipped recess to demonstrate she knew her times-tables through the 12s.

"Hey, Kallan?" I look up from my computer and the email response. "This punishment math ... did it look like multiplication tables?"

"Maybe." She can't help a burst of pride. "The teacher couldn't believe I knew them all!"

The next day, Kallan is hysterical over a handful of graded papers that have been returned with small curlicued red scribbles all over the pages. "Why does she hate me? Everything is marked in red! I'm failing everything! Everything I do is wrong! Look at all these red scribbles! She told me I am failing 3rd grade!"

Unable to figure out what the red scribbles mean, I email the teacher yet again, and she responds immediately, explaining that she took Kallan aside more than a week ago to inform Kallan that she needs to print her *k*s with a loop at the top, because that's how the kids in Oregon learned to make *k*s, and proper letter formation will assist Kallan in transitioning to cursive writing. She has only marked the corrections in red, she tells me, because

Kallan has had ample opportunity to address the small issue and refuses to do so.

I turn to Kallan, who is reading this email over my shoulder. "Mom, she is crushing my independent spirit! K is in my name every time I write it, and I don't want to do it her way. I like my *k*s how I do them. Why does she have to be so bossy?"

The next day, Kallan arrives home with a series of tearful complaints. "She said I can't be friends with the popular girls, and she moved my desk into a corner to isolate me, and she made me mop floors as a punishment for talking in class, and she said if I don't get my act together, I won't be allowed to go to high school."

I stare at Kallan. "Really? You want to stand by all of those statements?"

She wipes an actual tear from her cheek and looks up at me with mournful eyes. "You don't know how she is, Mom."

I send another email to Kallan's teacher, and she responds immediately, suggesting we meet in person.

.....

Later that evening, I return home from my meeting with the teacher, and I sink into the couch, exhausted. "Kallan is going to be the death of me."

Mark looks up from his computer. "What happened at the meeting?"

"Alright, so I've been telling you that Kallan has been coming home with all these stories, and that I keep emailing the teacher to be sure everything's alright ..."

"Yes."

"OK, well it was getting a little embarrassing, emailing every day with Kallan's version of events, but I couldn't just let her stories go." I sigh. "Maybe because we were doing the home-schooling ...

I just feel incredibly responsible for making Kallan's transition back to school go smoothly. When she tells me there's a problem, I can't just ignore it."

"And ..."

"And so this afternoon, after Kallan spun me yet another highly implausible story of teacher wrongdoing, I sent yet another email to the teacher, asking if there was a way for me to get a class-list of parent phone numbers, so that I could double-check Kallan's stories with parents before pestering the teacher every day."

"That sounds reasonable."

"It would have been, except in my email, I may have typed something like ... *If I had a list of parent phone numbers, I could more easily determine the truth from the lies when Kallan reports something to me that seems questionable.*"

Mark stares at me. "I must be missing something."

I slump sideways into the couch cushions. "The teacher read that to mean I thought **she** was lying about things, and that I wanted to be able to check with other parents about **her** possible lies and misbehavior."

Mark chokes on laughter and then continues laughing helplessly. "That is amazing. I wish I had been there ... this must have been the most awkward meeting in the history of the world."

"It really was. She was crying."

"Kallan's teacher cried? Oh my god, that's so awesome."

"And she barfed."

Mark is delighted. "In front of you?"

"No, but she told me about it, and when I hugged her, she smelled of vomit and fear."

"You hugged her? You don't hug people."

"Shut up. I had to."

Mark leans back in his chair, still laughing, "Best parent-teacher conference ever."

"It was a nightmare."

"I'm so glad I married you."

I mumble into a couch cushion, "What, because of my gift for awkward?"

He agrees happily. "It's like your best thing."

"Annoying."

A bit later, I lean to tuck Kallan into bed. I kiss her forehead. "Good night, sweetie."

Her eyes glow with a combination of horror and awe. "She really barfed?"

"She really did."

"And she cried? Because of you? Because you went in to talk to her about me? She cried?"

"She really did."

Kallan shudders with delight. "She was that scared of you?"

"I've heard reports I'm gifted at awkward ... sensible to be scared of a mother who can bring the awkward hammer down."

"I can't believe she was scared of you. I'm not scared of you."

"I know, right? I'm amazing! Know what I can't believe?"

"What?"

"That you were scared of her." I trace a finger along Kallan's cheek. "Because you know what? She's pretty amazing as well."

"You think?"

"I do. Know what else I think?"

"What?"

"That once you stop being scared of her, you'll stop feeling the need to make me see her as a monster."

Kallan snuggles under her blankets and giggles softly. "I can't believe she cried."

.....

Kallan arrives home from school the next day, and I ask, "How was school today?"

She throws her backpack on the counter and goes in search of a snack. "Fine."

"Just fine?"

She turns to stare at me. "Not every day is filled with drama and excitement, Mom. Some days are just good."

Good.

Spoiled hooker milk

The girls make friends quickly, which leads to plans for their very first sleepover guests in the new house. Somehow, these plans involve extracting repeated promises from me that I will do the laundry, because Maj and Kallan apparently each have only one exactly perfect sleepover outfit, and both of these outfits are dirty. They sit by the door, pulling on their shoes before heading out to the school-bus stop, and Maj says, for what seems like the hundredth time, "OK, so you promise to do the laundry while we're at school?"

"The sleepover isn't until tomorrow night," I point out, "so no ... once again ... I do not promise to do the laundry while you are at school. However, I do promise to do the laundry before your sleepover guests arrive."

Both girls pause in the tying of their shoelaces to stare up at me suspiciously. Kallan says, "This is important, Mom."

"I promise. I promise. Your jammies will be clean. Geez!"

Maj narrows her eyes at me. "OK, but they have to be clean by tomorrow night."

"I get it. Sleepover. Our house. Children must be clothed. No naked sleepovering. Seriously, ladies ... I've got it."

"You promise?"

"You are driving me crazy. I am a completely capable person, and I have been known to successfully usher dirty clothing through the washer and dryer and then back into your hands for wearing. Stop acting like I am perhaps the sort to get confused and eat the detergent."

"So is that a promise that the laundry will be done?"

I strike a dramatic pose and speak in my best superhero voice, "I AM MOTHER-MOM! WATCH ME LAUNDER IN A TIMELY FASHION!"

Neither girl seems reassured, and Kallan points out, "Ummmmm ... Mom? The power to wash laundry would be like the worst superpower EVER!"

I laugh as they gather up their backpacks. "Right? Motherhood comes with seriously lame superpowers and the worst costume ever." I wave my hands to indicate my outfit. "T-shirt and jeans ... how am I supposed to instill fear in this get-up?"

Kallan points. "Plus, your pants are unzipped."

I reach to zip them. "That's it. I am totally ordering an inertia belt to hold up these wonder-pants."

Maj whirls on me. "Inertia means not doing anything, but you're going to do the laundry, right?"

I pretend not to hear her; instead I unbutton and unzip my pants again and stare down into them ... "Wait, did the salesman say these were wonder-pants? Or was he inquiring about my underpants?" I look up at the girls cheerfully. "Being a superhero is sometimes confusing."

Kallan shakes her head. "Seriously, you are the worst superhero ever."

I put my hands on my hips, pants still slightly askew, and I use my superhero voice to loudly intone, "I AM MOTHER-MOM! I WILL KEEP THE HOUSE SAFE FROM ATTACK DURING YOUR

EDUCATIONAL ABSENCE! ALSO, I WILL EAT DETERGENT!"
As the school bus appears, the girls scurry away, shoulders hunched against the embarrassment of me. Still in superhero stance, I call out, "GO FORTH AND SUBDUE THE MASSES ... IN THE NAME OF MOTHER-MOM, SUBDUE THE UNWASHED MASSES!"

I sip my coffee and wave at the bus driver as my two daughter-minions fail in their attempts at invisibility. I watch as Kallan takes a seat near the front of the almost empty bus and Maj makes her way to the back. Maj has arrived at the new school as one of the big kids, and the big kids get to sit in the back of the bus. Younger kids have to sit in the front half of the bus. Maj is delighted with her status and the perks that come with it, but Kallan, who is accustomed to doing everything with her sister, is feeling left out. Kallan pulled me aside not long after they started school. "Could you please ask Maj to sit with me? She can move to the back after some other kids get on, but I hate that first part when I'm all alone in the front of the bus."

I tried to talk to Maj. "I understand that Kallan is not allowed to sit in the back of the bus, but would it kill you to sit with your sister in the front once in a while?"

Maj was adamant. "Yes, Mother. It totally would."

As the bus pulls away, I walk back into the house and sink into the couch, wishing Kallan was having an easier time of it, wishing Maj was a little more inclusive. I smile at the thought of the upcoming sleepover; if past experience is any indication, we will be hosting two separate sleepovers — one for Kallan and the two friends, and another for the sullen and potentially solo Maj, who will be yet again astounded to find that she is the only person in the entire world who does not find Kallan great fun to be around.

.....

The following evening, the laundry (and the vital sleepover outfits) washed and dried and folded and put away, Maj stands before me. "Mother, could you just tell Kallan to stop being so ... Kallan-ish? She's taking my friend." In the background, from the floor above, I can hear the shrieks and giggles and horrifying crashes that indicate Kallan has taken control of the sleepover.

"Listen, Maj. Kallan isn't trying to exclude you ... go join in the fun."

There is another enormous crash from above, and Maj frowns at me. "Do you know what they are doing? They are being elephant ballet dancers; that is literally the name of the so-called game: **Elephant Ballet-Dancers.**"

"Sounds like fun."

"And they are covered in glitter. Kallan's friend has glitter in her hair, and I don't imagine her mother is going to be very pleased about that."

"It's not a big deal."

"And they spilled water all over the bathroom with their imaginary trunks."

"Toss a towel down."

"So basically, you are useless as an authority figure, Mother?"

"Let me know if there is blood. As long as the screams are happy, leave me out of it."

"Mother, I want my friend back. Go get her for me."

"That's not how friends work, Maj."

"I would like my friend to behave as though she is my age. Go tell her that. Go tell her to free herself from Kallan's clutches."

"I will do no such thing."

"They are excluding me, Mother. I feel bullied and forlorn. Address my issues."

"You are neither bullied nor forlorn, and they are not excluding you. You are choosing not to join in the fun they are having."

"Whatever, Mother. This has been a very unsatisfactory conversation."

"You're welcome."

Maj stares at me darkly. "Just don't come whining to me when I take steps to address this problem, and it turns out you don't like the steps I have taken." She runs off, and I grab my book, only half-reading, waiting resignedly for the other shoe to drop, which it does, perhaps ten minutes later, in the form of a solitary and dejected Kallan. She comes wandering into the kitchen to ask for a piece of paper and some crayons. She sits down and starts drawing a picture.

She says nothing more, and so after a moment, I ask, "Sweetie, why aren't you playing with your friends?"

She answers without looking up from her coloring, "I'm **IT**."

"Like hide and seek IT? Shouldn't you be looking for them, then?"

Kallan sighs and looks up at me. "Maj made up a game called *Lights-Out Hide and Seek*. They turned off all the lights down in the basement, and they are hiding in the dark."

"Did you agree to play this game?"

"Yeah. I knew Maj was trying to come up with a game that I didn't want to play, and so I said I would play just to spite her, but ...,"she shrugs, "it's too dark and scary." She returns to her coloring. "So I'm just going to wait until they get tired of hiding and come out to find *me*."

"Why don't you just go around turning the lights back on?"

"Then they'll know I'm scared and think I'm a baby. Better they think I forgot about them." She outlines a big pink heart next to the dancing elephant she has drawn.

"So take your guide dog with you into the darkness." I leash up Jack the terrier and hand him over to Kallan. "He can help you find them."

Kallan agrees doubtfully, but she returns in less than a minute, dragging a seemingly dead dog behind her. Jack has no interest in helping. She hauls Jack to the middle of the kitchen and throws his leash down. "What kind of guide dog has to be dragged around the house on his back?" She glares at Jack, and he lies motionless on the floor, still harnessed and leashed, waiting for her to go away.

She bends to pet him. "It's OK, Jack. There's no reason you should be motivated to find children in the dark; it's not like I'm asking you to find hiding hamburgers. You would be an excellent guide dog if your job was to help me find hiding hamburgers."

I think for a minute, and then I yell out, "Come out, come out, wherever you are ... time for cookies!" In an instant, there is the sound of three girls tumbling up the stairs and out of the basement darkness. I hand them each a cookie, and then I make a show of holding Kallan back as I hand Kallan her cookie. "You guys go back to your hiding spots ... take your cookies with you ... Kallan will come find you in a minute."

Maj sneers, "Will she, though? Because last I checked, Kallan is afraid of the dark."

My tone casually innocent, I ask, "I meant to ask ... how are you doing sleeping under the training wheels of death, anyway?"

All four girls turn to look at me, and Maj asks, "What?"

"You know, the trains painted on your bedroom walls. I know you were concerned they were demon trains ... *ghost trains of death*, I believe you called them."

Maj's friend looks at Maj. "Is she talking about the **Thomas the Train** paintings on your wall?"

Maj glares at me before answering her friend. "I'm not scared of the trains. My mother is insane most of the time. Disregard everything she says from this point forward."

Kallan giggles. "Training wheels of death ... that's awesome!" She bounces happily in the air. "Hey, I have a great idea! Let's all have awesome secret nicknames that no one but us will know!"

The friends are eagerly on board with this plan. Quickly, it emerges that one of the girls has always wanted to be called Apostrophe, and Kallan assigns the other girl the nickname Handbasket. Maj is incredulous. "Seriously? I'm supposed to call you guys Apostrophe and Handbasket?" Apostrophe and Handbasket nod their heads happily.

Kallan is delighted. "And I will be called Pajaro, after the street we used to live on."

Maj doesn't want to be left out, and so, annoyed with herself for cooperating, she relents. "Fine. Apostrophe, Handbasket, and Pajaro ... what's my nickname?"

Kallan's eyes widen at her sister's confusion. "You already have a nickname. Mom gave it to you."

"You mean ..."

Kallan grabs the shoulders of the three girls, one girl at a time, and lines them up for presentation. "Mom, this is Apostrophe. This is Handbasket. I am Pajaro. And this is my sister, who is known as Training Wheels of Death."

Maj is, for once, utterly speechless. After that moment passes, however, her features harden, and she says, "Alright, then ... it's back to *Lights-Out Hide and Seek*. Kallan, you're still **IT**."

I hand another cookie to each fleeing girl, holding the cookies high to keep them out of Jack's leaping jaws, and then I bend to whisper in Kallan's ear. "After you count to 20, take Jack with you to find them ... he'll be more helpful now that cookies are hiding."

She nods and takes a frenzied cookie-starved Jack's leash. She finishes counting ... "17, 18, 19, 20 ... Here I come, ready or not!"

Jack drags her down the stairs into the darkness to hunt cookies.

Apostrophe ... FOUND!

Handbasket ... FOUND!

Training Wheels of Death ... FOUND!

And then Kallan/Pajaro's happy voice. "Hey, you guys want to do makeovers and then climb out onto the garage roof for a runway show?"

All but Training Wheels of Death are thrilled with this plan. I yell out, "No runway roof shows!" but I get only disobedient giggling in response. Training Wheels of Death appears before me, alone and sullen. "**YOU KNOW I HATE MAKEUP, MOTHER.** Tell the one that is mine that it's time for bed."

"You mean Apostrophe?"

She rolls her eyes. "Whatever. Yes, tell Apostrophe it's time for her to go to bed."

"It's 7:30, and I'm doing no such thing."

Training Wheels of Death throws herself onto the couch. "**I WAS MEANT TO BE AN ONLY CHILD, MOTHER. YOU'VE MESSED UP THE ENTIRETY OF MY EXISTENCE BY BIRTHING A SECONDARY CHILD.**"

"Messing up the entirety of your existence is pretty much what I live for, babe."

"Very funny, Mother." Maj waits for a moment in case I have plans to improve her situation, but when I do nothing at all, she takes a deep breath and heads up the stairs. I listen as she ascends, yelling as she goes, "**ALRIGHT I'LL DO MAKEUP BUT THERE WILL BE NO SMOKY EYES, DO YOU HEAR**

ME? NO ONE IS SMOKING MY EYEBALLS!" She is greeted with giggle-shrieks. "**OH MY GOSH ... ARE YOU HUGGING ME? I DON'T DO HUGS. YOU ALL LOOK LIKE HOOKERS. WAS THAT THE GOAL? BECAUSE IF SO, WELL DONE, I MUST SAY. What? WHAT ARE YOU DOING? GET AWAY FROM ME!**"

A few minutes later, Training Wheels of Death comes stomping back down the stairs, her lips a vividly painted bow of red, her eyes smoky as a forest fire. "Not a word about this beauty ambush, Mother. Not ... one ... word."

I hold out the plate. "Cookie?"

She takes a cookie. "Monday at school I'm going to need to find my people."

"What about Apostrophe?"

"You mean Darcy? Kallan's got her, and anyway, look how easily she turned ... like spoiled hooker milk."

I stare at her. "Remember that thing I said before about living to mess up your existence?"

"Yes." She takes a bite of cookie. "What about it?"

"I was wrong. What I in fact live for are things like *spoiled hooker milk*. That's magical."

She smiles, a very small smile, at the thought. "You are an odd woman, Mother."

"Totally am."

From upstairs, I hear the sound of a bedroom window sliding open.

Ack.

Runway shows of doom

"Hey, Maj?"

"Yeah?"

"You know your smaller frog Big, the one-eyed frog?"

"I only have two frogs, Mother. Chances are I know which one is the smaller frog named Big who has one eye."

"Sorry. It's just ... I know I said that he would be fine, but I think the journey up here was more difficult for him than I imagined it would be, and ..."

Maj puts up a hand. "Stop talking, Mother."

"It's just ... I was in your room a few minutes ago, and Big is looking all wrinkly and hollow. I know you've been force-feeding him crickets ..."

"Mother, he's been tired, and with only one good eye, sometimes it's hard for him to find the crickets. I haven't been force-feeding Big; I have been assisting him."

"All I'm trying to say is that he doesn't look good, and I think you should prepare yourself ..."

"No, Mother. I refuse to be prepared. Being prepared is an

invitation for the bad thing to happen, because the bad thing can see that you have already done the work of complacency and acceptance. No, if the bad thing is coming, it is going to have to shove me and my angry denial out of the way to get to Big."

The next day, Maj arrives home from school and disappears into her room for a short moment of silence that is then shattered like too-thin ice over depth.

"AIAIEIEIEIEEEIIEIEIEEEEE!"

Inhale ...

"AIAIEIEIEIEEEIIEIEIEEEEE!"

Inhale ...

"AIAIEIEIEIEEEIIEIEIEEEEE!"

I make my way up the stairs and into Maj's room, where she is staring wild-eyed into her frogs' terrarium. Little the bigger two-eyed frog is green and round and wishing he had a quieter owner; he blinks his eyes angrily against the vibratory assault of Maj's screams. Below his branched perch rests the smaller one-eyed frog Big, who is very and undeniably dead. I lean in to look at him. "He looks like he died mid-leap."

Maj speaks through tears, "No, Mother. When I came in, Big was curled up by the pond, all quiet and peaceful. I didn't think he was dead, but he did look weirdly still, so I picked him up and put him on his favorite branch." She turns to me. "You know, to encourage him to look around a little bit." She wails, "Except he wouldn't balance, and when I let go of him, he just rolled off the branch ... and even as he fell, I was thinking he was such a good-boy frog, doing some sort of fancy jump, except then he just fell in a heap, and his arms and legs stretched out as far as they could go like he was reaching for something and look at him, Mother, **LOOK AT HIM!**"

The frog is lying on his back in the moss, all four of his legs extended. He looks for all the world like a teeny dead suicide leaper, his pale belly bloated and his naked limbs extended in absolute surrender. I reach to scoop him up, and I tuck his legs up under his body; I present him to Maj in my outstretched palm. "I'm sorry, Maj. I know frogs are sensitive ... I did the best I could with the move. I really did."

Maj tentatively caresses the frog's body with a single finger, and then she takes him from me and tucks him up against her tear-stained cheek. "I will miss you, Big."

"You were a very good owner to Big, Maj."

Maj holds the dead frog out to the live frog, who remains perched on his branch. "Look, Little ... Big is gone. What?" She pretends to listen to Little's thoughts, and then she shakes her head in exasperation. "No, we will not be getting you a new frog-friend this afternoon. A period of mourning is required. Have a bit of decency, Little." She holds the dead frog in front of her face and stares at him assessingly. "Little has a point, though ... this really doesn't even look like Big anymore. Whatever was in there that made Big himself is gone." She returns her attention to Little's disrespect. "That doesn't give you the right to start making replacement plans. His body's hardly even cold ... what?" She cocks her head incredulously. "Little, I know you did not just make a joke about amphibian body-temperature in this time of great sorrow. Perhaps you should hush up."

Little the still-living frog blinks at Maj several times and apparently makes promises to stop being so insensitive, because Maj nods her head. "Alright, then." She turns back to me. "Do we have a small Tupperware container I could use as a frog-casket? I'll keep him in the refrigerator for a few days, and we'll bury him when Kallan's not home." Maj is distracted by a request from Little the living frog, and she listens for a few seconds and then chastises him, "No. No, you may not have his dead decaying body as a fly attractant. **WHAT IS WRONG WITH YOU?**" She turns back to me. "I want to bury Big in the back yard, but if I do it when Kallan's home, she'll just go out there and dig him back up again to see how the dead is going."

I start to protest on Kallan's behalf, but Maj waves me off, the dead frog riding along on the arc of her palm's dismissal. "Mother, she still has Shelly's corpse. She packed up his dead body like it was jewelry and brought him with us from California. She checks on him every few days to see how he's doing. He's always dead, but still she wants to see what's different from the last time he was dead. Mother, you know she would dig up Big if she could ... you know she would."

Shelly was a companion turtle to Delilah who died within days of arriving at our home, when he was still just the size of a fifty-cent piece. "She brought Shelly with her? I don't think so ... she buried Shelly by the pathway of our house in Vallejo."

Maj looks at me pityingly. "Shelly's in Kallan's room."

"Really?"

"Really."

"Huh ... OK, so Big's funeral will be done in secrecy."

"Thank you, Mother."

At this moment, Kallan comes rushing into the room, breathless and red-cheeked. She is about to speak, but she notices Maj making concealing motions, and she switches gears, craning her neck to try to see around Maj's back. "What are you hiding?"

Maj thinks for a few seconds and comes up with, "Nothing."

Kallan rolls her eyes. "You are like the worst liar in the entire world. Whatever you're hiding, you know I'm going to find out eventually. All I have to do is keep asking you until you break." Maj not-so-surreptitiously wipes at her eyes with her empty hand, and Kallan's eyes widen. "Are you crying?"

"I am not crying. I am not hiding anything, I'm not crying, and **I CAN TOO KEEP A SECRET, YOUNG LADY.**"

Kallan considers for a moment, and then she takes a step closer to her sister. "What are you hiding?"

"Big the Frog." Maj holds out her hand to show her sister the small curled-up deadness.

"Oh for goodness sake ... that's the worst secret ever. Why do you even have secrets if they are going to be so lame and why are you crying and holding a frog?"

Maj realizes that her sister doesn't understand the frog she is holding is dead, and she takes a second, and comes up with, "Big peed in my eyes. It stings."

Kallan snorts with laughter. "That is the worst lie ever. Go ahead and have your secret, but don't insult me. If a frog had peed in your eyes, you would be running around the house screaming at the top of your lungs, and you would not be lovingly cradling the offending frog." Kallan laughs again. "Seriously, Maj ... you are the worst liar ever. You need to pay attention — you could learn a thing or two from me." Kallan turns to me. "OK, so Mom?"

Maj takes this opportunity to duck out of the room with her frog, presumably in search of a casket, and I say to Kallan, "Uh oh."

Kallan speaks soothingly, "Mom, there's no need to be scared."

"Uh oh again."

"Alright, you know how the girl next door found like a swarm of salamanders in her back yard when she was digging her slave-tunnel, and she gave me two of them?"

"Yes."

"I was keeping them in a little box in my room. I gave them moss and water and dirt and worms, and they seemed happy enough." She corrects herself, "Well, maybe they weren't thrilled, because they kept trying to escape the shoe-box. I could hear them at night scrabbling against the cardboard limits for a way out. Except last night, they didn't scrabble, and so I went to bed thinking that they had finally accepted me as their god, and I was a tiny bit happy that I had trained them to behave, but turns out ... not so much." She reaches into her pocket and pulls out her pets. "Turns out they weren't trained at all. They're dead," she announces sadly as she shakes them back and forth by their tails to demonstrate the cooperative and docile nature of dead salamanders. She holds them high in front of her face and addresses them crankily, "This is not how I imagined accepting me as your god would look."

I sigh and explain, "Wild animals sometimes don't do so well when you try to make them into pets. Next time, leave the salamanders to do their own lives out in the wild instead of asking them to be shoe-box pets."

"No, I don't think they minded being pets," she says as she tucks the dead animals back into her pocket, "I just think that last fashion runway show was one too many for them."

I cringe. "Salamander fashion-runway shows?"

Kallan meets my eyes. "Here's where you have to ask yourself, Mom ... do you really want to know or not?"

"If I say I don't want to know, can we agree that there will be no more wildlife runway shows of doom?"

"Agreed."

"Alright ... next topic."

Kallan considers. "How about a slightly related topic? I need you to talk to my teacher again, because she is sucking all the kill-joy out of History."

"She is sucking the kill-joy? I need to write this stuff down."

"Mom, I'm being serious. All she talks about is the Oregon Trail. People here in Oregon are obsessed with the Oregon Trail, were you aware? It's like nothing else in history matters ... thousands of years of perfectly fascinating blood and gore and evil, and what are we learning? We're learning about stupidly unprepared people making journeys in covered wagons. It's super boring, but you know me ... I always look for the bright side of things."

"And the bright side of the Oregon Trail is ..."

Kallan is surprised at the question. "Death and disease and horror, obviously. Did you know that people died of dysentery, which is a fancy way of saying they diarrhea-ed themselves to death?" Kallan hugs herself and her salamander corpses joyfully. "And sometimes? They just threw the poo-covered dead people out of the covered wagons and left the bodies for the vultures."

"And so you mentioned this news in class?"

"Yes, and the teacher said I have a tendency toward the ... hold on ... it was a fancy word ...," Kallan thinks back, " ... *ma-cobbler*, maybe?"

"*Macabre*. It means dark and gruesome and perhaps a bit too attentive to the details of death."

Kallan nods, happy to have cleared this up. "That's alright, then."

"I'm guessing your teacher would prefer if you didn't relish the details of poo-covered dead people cast beside the roadway quite as much as you do."

"That's pretty much what she said, word for word. So I need you to talk to her. Explain about History being all about death." She switches gears. "Oh, and also, I have a book report to do, and my teacher said I need to learn how to take direction better, which is her way of saying I'm not doing the book reports her way, and so she gave me an outline to follow, and she said you need to sign my report before I turn it in."

"Have you read the book?"

"Yup."

"When's it due?"

Kallan cocks her head. "Tuesday? Wednesday? One of the days with *day* in it."

"OK, so we'll work on that over the weekend."

"Sounds good." Kallan dances across her sister's room to look in the terrarium. "Tell Maj I'm sorry Big died."

"So you did notice."

"Yeah, but she was sad ... I like to pester Maj, but not when she's sad, so I didn't say anything."

"You're a good sister."

"I know, right?" She dances back to me and pulls out the limp salamanders again. "Do you think Maj wants to do a mass grave?"

"I'm betting not."

She swings them by their tails. "Poor salamanders ... beauty is cruel."

"I don't want to know."

Kallan runs from the room, cackling wildly.

Maj returns, her frog ensconced in Tupperware, her eyes red. "Hey, Mother?"

"Yes, babe?"

"I know I said that I would blame you if Big died, but it's not your fault. There was no way to leave him behind, but it turns out there was no way to bring him along either. I know you did the best you could."

Kallan leaps back into the room. "OH MY GOSH, THAT'S EXACTLY WHAT THE FAMILIES SAID AS THEY TOSSED THEIR DEAD RELATIVES OUT OF THE COVERED WAGONS! Maj, is there ANY way I can borrow Big's body for a presentation on the Oregon Trail? I promise promise promise that when I'm done with him, I'll wipe off the poo." She waits for an answer, her face alight with enthusiasm.

Maj hugs her Tupperwared frog to her chest and shrieks in horror.

Kallan sighs. "So that's a no?"

Warble-booty

It has been gorgeous here for the past few days, a sort of mini-spring that people warn me will soon end in a deluge of rain and mud, and so we have been spending a lot of time in the back yard, trying to enjoy the lovely weather while it lasts. The girls are digging a hole. Not for the frog and salamanders ... no ... all of the dead amphibians are Tupperware-sealed in the downstairs freezer. No, what started out as a pool for slugs (who turned out to be spectacularly ungrateful and stubbornly resistant to swimming) has become a much bigger plan to lure neighborhood children or possibly their own mother into broken-legged doom. Maj and Kallan have been taking turns preparing the hole, which is just wide enough for one girl with a small shovel to stand within and dig ... a little bit wider than a manhole cover, perhaps. Their plan is to dig the hole deep enough that a hapless victim will fall through branches and leaves laid cunningly over the entrance and then said hapless victim will disappear from view. The girls are giddy at the thought.

They are also very proud of their hole, and so everyone in the neighborhood has been called over to appreciate its mighty killing power. This lack of secrecy and stealth has somewhat diminished their chances of catching anything other than a very stupid neighborhood child, but when I point this out, the girls are unconcerned. Maj assures me, "Mother, even genius falls if you push it." Kallan nods agreement.

I stare at them. "OK, then. I don't know what I was thinking. Carry on."

Progress, however, has been slow and fraught with peril. The hole is in the far corner of the yard, and after several days of digging, the girls thought to look up, where they discovered a tangled swing caught in the branches of the elm tree whose roots they had been struggling to chop. Once the swing was freed, it gave the girl who was not shoveling something to do while she waited for her turn. Except ... the swing's path is directly over the hole, and so every arc of the swing is a new opportunity for serious injury.

"Maj, I am shoveling. You can't swing when I am shoveling. You are going to kill me."

Maj is unconcerned as she swings over her sister, who has to crouch low beneath the swing's path to avoid being kicked in the head. "The hole's big enough; just shovel in between my swings and duck down when I come by."

Kallan is invisible to me now, but I can hear her voice as she yells up at her sister. "Are you kidding me right now? How am I supposed to know when it's safe to come out? Stop swinging!"

"If I stop swinging, I don't have anything to do," Maj responds reasonably as she extends her feet as hard and high as she can. "Here's what I'll do for you ... I'll go super high, and that will give you more time between swings to do the digging."

Kallan is still tucked low in the hole, and she yells, "That's genius, Maj. Why don't I just poke my head up and have it be kicked off my body like a football?"

Maj leans to look down into the hole as she swings. She informs her sister, "You are making like zero progress."

"AUGH! If you don't stop swinging right this instant, I am going to lift the shovel up into your path, and then we'll see what's lopped off."

"OH MY GOSH, MOTHER! MOTHER!" Maj leaps from the swing mid-arc and tumbles into the ivy beyond the hole. **"MOTHER! KALLAN IS THREATENING TO KILL ME WITH A SHOVEL! SHE SERIOUSLY JUST CROUCHED**

HERE UNDERNEATH ME AND SAID SHE WOULD KILL ME WITH A SHOVEL!"

Kallan emerges grim-faced from the hole, shovel in hand. "Maj, you are a lunatic."

They both stare at me from across the yard, but when I do nothing but wave and sip my coffee, they soon return to the task at hand. Maj steps into the hole. "Hand me the shovel, Kallan ... it's my turn to dig." Kallan stands and watches her sister toss out a few small shovels of dirt, and then she settles herself in the swing.

"Watch out, Maj!" Kallan lifts her feet to just barely pass above her sister's head. Maj lifts her face in alarm and then shrieks as she throws herself into the hole.

"WE ALREADY SETTLED HOW DANGEROUS THE SWING IS. STOP SWINGING RIGHT THIS INSTANT! LEARN FROM MY MISTAKES, YOUNG LADY! I DEMAND COMPLIANCE WITH MY DEMANDS!"

"Here's what I'll do for you, Maj. I'll pump super hard and go super high, and that will give you just enough time to shovel in between the beheading opportunities."

"OH ... MY ... GOSH. WHEN I GET OUT OF THIS HOLE, I AM GOING TO KILL YOU."

Kallan swings happily. "The thing about swinging, though, is that it is the sort of activity I could do for hours and hours."

"FINE, I'LL JUST LOP OFF YOUR FEET WITH THE SHOVEL, JUST LIKE YOU WERE GOING TO DO TO ME."

Kallan leans mid-swing to stare down at her huddled sister. "The difference between you and me, Maj? Is your inability to dismiss empty threats."

"DANG IT DANG IT DANG IT YOU CANNOT RENDER ME POWERLESS AND CAPTIVE. I WILL NOT STAND FOR IT!"

"Standing is probably not your best move," Kallan agrees as she powers into another ascent.

"MOTHER! MOTHER, GET YOUR BUTT OUT HERE AND SAVE YOUR OLDER DAUGHTER'S LIFE! I AM TRAPPED IN A HOLE AND I DEMAND RESCUE AND THEN I ALSO DEMAND THAT THE SHE-DEMON AGGRESSOR BE PUNISHED SEVERELY. I'M THINKING FLOGGING, MOTHER ... NO, I AM DEMANDING SHE BE FLOGGED. GET OUT HERE WITH YOUR FLOGGING TOOLS, MOTHER!"

Instead of fetching my flogging tools, I head to the freezer and grab two ice-cream bars, which I wave at Kallan. Kallan comes flying across the yard as though she's in fast-forward; it takes Maj a moment to realize the coast is clear, and then she scrambles up and out of the hole to come get an ice cream. I hold Maj's treat high above my head. "You can only have this if you promise I don't have to hear anything about how you were almost killed."

She relents. "OK, but I was almost killed. I would like that on the record, even if I am not going to have an opportunity to detail the savagery."

Kallan licks her ice cream a few times and then wonders aloud, "Hey, Maj? How come you are always so concerned with safety, but then you and I do things together like dig holes underneath swings?"

Maj considers as she eats her own ice cream. "I blame you. You are a bad influence on me." Kallan accepts this explanation without question, and Maj turns to me. "Mother, while we are standing here discussing the dangers I am willing to undertake, I would like you to explain to me again why I cannot have a climbing rope."

Before I can answer, a face appears over the fence at the side of the yard, and Kallan waves the face's owner into our yard. The neighbor girl clamors over the fence and walks to stand silently before me, playing a mime-version of "Which of these things is not like the other?" I take a stab in the dark. "Would you like an ice cream cone?" The girl nods, and then, ice cream in hand, she and Kallan head off to the back of the yard and start climbing the fence. Maj and I watch as the girls start waving their arms and yelling mild insults into the two yards beyond our property in the rear.

I ask Maj, "What is your sister doing?"

"She's trying to make friends with the kids who live in the two houses behind us."

"But aren't those the boys Kallan hates? The ones who run around the neighborhood screaming and pretending to shoot everyone?"

"Yup. Kallan has decided she wants them to like her."

Kallan and her friend are now throwing small rocks and sticks into the yards behind our fence. I listen. I am pretty sure Kallan just called someone a "warble-booty," which seems an odd flirtation. I look at Maj, waiting for better answers.

Maj finishes the last of her ice cream. She shrugs. "Kallan found out they have pools in their back yards. When summer gets here, Kallan wants to know and be loved by the people with pools."

"Ahhhhh. That makes sense. But what about you? You're not interested?"

"Mother, those boys are hideous. If I don't like someone outside of a pool, what's going to change to make it so much fun to be *in* a pool with them?"

"You are so very you, Maj. Always."

Maj is suspicious. "Is that a compliment?"

"Definitely."

Mark opens the back door to let out the two dogs — one regularly collared Labrador and one terrier wearing a plastic medical cone. Persie the Labrador lumbers off into the ivy in search of privacy, and Jack sits at my feet, annoyed he has missed out on ice cream. He stares up at me balefully, his face surrounded by a very un-angelic halo of festive purple plastic. I reach into the cone to scratch his ears. "Hold on, Jack. I'll get you a treat."

I return in a moment with a handful of kibble. I toss it piece by piece to Jack, who has never been good at catching thrown treats. However, he has learned that his new collar offers certain advantages; he sits very still and offers his collar as a huge target; treats fall down into the cone and collect around his neck. When he is certain that all the treats have been tossed, he whips his head down so that the cone seals against the ground; all the treats fall to the ground within that secret protected circle. I laugh. "Jack, you are a genius in your stupidity."

Maj sighs. "When can he stop wearing that collar? He looks ridiculous."

"He can stop wearing this collar as soon as you agree to run chicken-wire along the bottom of the fence around the entire yard."

Maj addresses the dog, "Sorry, Jack. I tried." She picks up the thread of conversation she abandoned earlier. "So about that climbing rope ..."

"The climbing rope you want me to hang from the tallest tree in our back yard so that you can climb ... I believe you said ... *higher than the rooftops* ... that climbing rope?"

"Yes."

"Let me ask you a few questions."

"Go ahead."

"Are you the same girl who tripped on the rug this morning?"

"That has nothing to do with climbing."

"And are you the same girl who crashed her shoulder into a door-frame and then claimed that the door had been moved while she was at school?"

"There are no doors on ropes, Mother."

"And are you the girl who regularly misses the last step because you claim there are twelve stairs when there are in fact thirteen?"

"Thirteen is an unlucky number. I refuse to acknowledge that last stair."

"And are you the girl who slipped in dog drool this morning and skated across the room before collapsing into a spectacular heap?"

"I could have been killed."

"And are you the girl who once simply walked away from a tug-of-war contest because you said the rope was burning you?"

"Obviously, we wouldn't buy the hot rope, Mother."

"And are you the girl who climbs trees all the time?"

"Wait, that last one's not me at all. I hate climbing trees."

"My point exactly."

"Mother, climbing trees and climbing ropes are entirely different things. Besides, if I wanted to climb a tree, I could climb a tree."

"Go do that, then."

"You're telling me to climb a tree? Is that what you are saying, Mother?"

"I would very much like to see you climb a tree."

"And then you'll buy me a climbing rope?"

"No. And then you'll be a girl who doesn't need a rope, because she knows how to climb trees."

Maj stares at me in challenge, her hands on her hips. "I will climb a tree, but if I am very good at climbing that tree, will you at least consider the climbing-rope thing?"

"Deal, uncoordinated child who didn't learn to skip until second grade."

"Don't sass me, Mother."

Maj runs off into the house. I call after her, "Maj, where are you going?"

"I need to change into my climbing outfit, Mother. Obviously."

"Obviously."

Having finished his treats, Jack the terrier heads off into the ivy to poo; he bounces delightedly through the undergrowth looking for the perfect spot; every time he sniffs the ground, he has to maneuver his cone into proper position, but he doesn't seem to mind. I sigh ... both of the dogs seem determined to hide their poo within the thick ivy-ed areas of the yard, making recovery difficult. Because the tangled dense ivy doesn't invite people exploration, I have mostly been allowing the poo to fill in the empty spaces beneath the green. Who's going to know?

Kallan and her friend are back, this time in need of Ziploc bags in which to collect slugs. I hand out bags and instructions. "OK, but when you're done appreciating the slugs, release them back into the wild, please." The girls agree.

And then Maj is back as well, dressed in shorts and a t-shirt and a long flowing scarf that she tosses dramatically over her shoulder as she announces, "I am off to conquer a tree." I watch as she assesses her options, which include several towering Sequoia, Elms, a few smaller pine trees, and a very small plum tree with only a few branches sturdy enough to support her weight. She chooses the plum tree, which overhangs the deck.

I smile as she stands next to the tree and reaches to test the strength of the first branch. "Aim high, babe."

"Mother, this is a tree. You said to climb a tree. You did not say I had to climb a huge tree."

I settle myself in a deck chair to watch her efforts.

The dogs are following the two younger girls around the yard, unsure about the plan but eager to be involved. The girls head off into the ivy, and then deeper into the ivy, and I call them over. "Hey, ladies? How about you search for slugs in the grass and the vegetable garden?"

They are immediately whiny, and Kallan speaks, "But Mom, the slugs we want are all in the ivy."

I hesitate, but then I say, "Here's the thing ... the dogs have been going potty in the ivy, and I don't want you guys stepping in poo."

The girls look at me incredulously, and Kallan says, "But we're having a contest to see who can find the biggest slugs."

I'm confused. "Why would the biggest slugs be in the ivy? There's plenty of fabulous yard for the big slugs to wander."

Kallan shakes her head. "No, Mom. You don't understand. The biggest slugs are the ones who settle in to eat the best meals."

"How is ivy a better meal than a dying vegetable garden?"

"Mom, listen." Kallan speaks very slowly, as though I have perhaps suffered a head injury that is impeding my comprehension, "The biggest slugs are the ones eating dog poo."

"Ewwwwww ... so you guys are hunting dog poo?"

"Duh."

"And then plucking slugs off the dog poo?"

"Again ... duh."

"With your bare hands?"

"We use sticks to separate the big-boy slugs from the poo they're hugging." Kallan explains as she and her friend hold up Ziploc bags of slugs, "We take off points if our bags end up with poo in them."

"OH MY GOSH, MOTHER. DO YOU HEAR WHAT THEY ARE SAYING? DO ... YOU ... COMPREHEND ... THE ... HORROR?"

"Hush, Maj." Maj's love affair with the slugs ended shortly after our arrival when her research revealed that during mating, the Banana Slug unsheathes a penis as long as the slug itself from a hole in its head. **"A HUGE PENIS COMES OUT OF ITS HEAD, MOTHER! WHAT ELSE IS THERE TO SAY?"**

I look at the neighbor girl. "Poo-hugging big-boy slugs? Seriously?"

The neighbor girl nods.

"Ugh. How about if you promise not to tell your mother how you spent your afternoon?" The neighbor girl nods. Behind the girls, Maj takes her first actual step up into the plum tree and lets out a little shriek of terror. I ignore the shrieking and I say to the neighbor girl, "Let's practice. I'll be your mom, and I say, *'Did you have a good time at Kallan's house?'* and then you say ..."

The girl whispers, "Yes."

"I'm still your mom, and I say, *'What did you guys do?'* and then you say ..." The neighbor girl is stymied, and she looks at me blankly. I try again. "The only wrong answer is *'Kallan and I spent the day plucking huge juicy slugs off dog poo.'* Anything other than that is fine."

The little girl thinks and then she whispers in Kallan's ear, and Kallan giggles. Kallan informs me, "She says if her mom asks, she'll say that she spent the afternoon hiding in a hole with a shovel while I threatened to kick her head off from a swing."

I smile in approval. "That's perfect."

Kallan and her friend run shrieking to the back of the yard, where Kallan stands at the fence and loudly wonders if "warble-booty" might like to have some slugs thrown at his head. Warble-booty is not so inclined, and he throws a slug into our yard to emphasize the point. The slug war commences.

I turn back to Maj, who is now hanging like a tragic monkey from the lowest plum-tree branch; her arms and legs are wrapped around the branch, and her butt is hanging low. "And I doubted you," I say apologetically, "You must be feeling pretty vindicated right about now."

Her teeth clenched and her cheeks red with effort, Maj growls at me as she clings to the branch. "Hush, Mother. Give me a second, and I will silence your doubts." With a grunt, she swings her body just enough to grab the next highest branch with her right hand. She starts trying to pull herself up, but her long silken scarf gets tangled in her feet, impeding her progress. Instead of working out a way to untangle the scarf, Maj stubbornly continues her ascent, causing the scarf to slowly tighten on her neck, pulling her into a weird fetal position as she climbs.

"Extreme sports are maybe not your forte, Maj," I observe.

I watch in disbelief as she slowly chokes herself. Eventually, after being strangled into a very tight scarfed curl of surrender, she releases her hold and falls from the tree. As it is a small tree, the fall is more of a graceless three-foot tumble into the unraked leaves below. I walk to stare down at her; she gasps for breath. "Hey, Maj?"

"Yes, Mother?"

"No way you are getting a climbing rope. No ... way."

She rolls onto her back and stares up at me sadly from the leaves, which appear to be intentionally tangling themselves in her hair. She loosens the scarf from around her neck. "Nature hates me."

Kallan and her friend come racing across the yard, fleeing a small gang of fence-scaling boys and screaming at the top of their lungs — a single word of warning: "IN ... COM ... ING!"

The air is alive with slugs.

The airborne slugs hit the ground and the deck and tree branches and the earth. They're like soldiers catapulted into battle, except having arrived at the battle, these particular soldiers decide they are done with the mission: they rest wetly where they land, considering their nonviolent options.

Splat ... splat ... splat.

"OH MY GOSH THERE IS A SLUG ON MY FACE! MOTHER, THERE IS A SLUG SUCKING MY FACE! GET HIM OFF OF ME! IS THIS ONE OF THE POO-SLUGS? THIS BETTER NOT BE ONE OF THE PENIS-HEAD POO SLUGS BECAUSE IF THIS IS ONE OF THE BIG-BOY PENIS-HEAD POO-HUGGING SLUGS, I AM GOING TO KILL ALL OF YOU."

I bend to scrape the slimy confused paratrooper from Maj's cheek. I pluck another from her hair. And another.

She struggles to her feet, somehow stepping on the end of the scarf as she does so, and she says, as she works to gain leverage, "Maybe I could have a climbing rope in my room ... you know ... where nature can't get me." The effectiveness of this proposal is hampered by the fact that she is speaking the words from a sort of weird bondage position in which the scarf is strangling her into a crouch. She tilts her face to look up at me. "What if I promise to never wear a scarf while climbing?"

"Not even."

"Way to glory in arbitrary power, Mother," Maj says as she tries and fails to untangle herself from the scarf. She tilts her head to glare at me. "I wouldn't be wearing this scarf when I climbed the rope, Mother." She whips her hands at the scarf and takes another step, which sends her crashing and stumbling to the ground, still with the throttling scarf around her neck. Maj claws at her neck until the scarf surrenders its grip, and then she flings it away from herself and looks up at me hopefully. "I mean ... who would be stupid enough to wear a long scarf when climbing, am I right?"

So right.

Tuck

I am sitting at my computer when Kallan comes to find me, waving a paper in her hand. "Alright, about this book report thing. My teacher says I have to do it her way, but her way is lame and so I refuse. I'm thinking of going on a hunger strike."

"You do know a hunger strike involves not eating, correct?"

Kallan alters course without pause, "OK, so no hunger strike. I'm making posters, though. There's going to be angry marching in the streets, I can tell you that." She takes a breath. "Do we have Sharpies and cardboard? I'm going to need Sharpies and cardboard!"

Maj looks up from her book. "Planning on being a homeless panhandler instead of a third-grader? Good plan ... you're poor student material, anyway. Everyone says so."

Kallan balls her fists in anger. "I am not poor student material! No one says that!"

"Pretty sure that's the word on the street."

"No, it is not." Kallan turns to me. "Make Maj stop talking."

Maj muses, "Ironic that once you're homeless and on the street, you'll be better positioned to hear the word on the street, which ... I promise you ... is that you're poor student material."

I point up the stairs. "Maj, go away. You are not being at all helpful."

"Whatever, Mother. I just speak the truth."

Kallan wails, "I am not poor student material!"

"For god's sake, of course you're not." I point again. "Go away, Maj. Go help your dad make dinner or something."

"Whatever, Mother. Maybe I'll go collect change to throw to Kallan when we pass her on the freeway exit."

Kallan walks to yell up the stairs, "If you collect change, I am not above accepting donations for the cause!" She turns back to me. "About this book report: I'm not doing it."

"Don't be silly. Of course you are."

She waves the paper again and then collects herself to read to me. "Listen to what it says. Listen to the assignment." She clears her throat and speaks officially, *"Write a short review of this book that focuses on its inspirational elements. Imagine you are recommending this book to a friend ... what parts of the story might your friend especially enjoy? Why are you recommending this book? What specifically makes it an enjoyable read? Make your review come alive with examples from the text, and be sure to share your thoughts about your favorite characters/parts of the story."*

I smile. "OK, the wording is a little flowery, but the assignment itself doesn't sound so difficult."

"Mom, did you even listen? I'm supposed to write a review, but I'm also supposed to recommend the book to a friend."

I hazard a guess. "So you didn't like the book?"

She shakes her head vehemently. "I hated it."

I take the paper from her hand and read it myself. "Huh. You're right. It doesn't leave room for hating the book, does it?"

Kallan flops dramatically to the floor and rolls about in frustration. "When you were in charge of the books, you always picked books I loved. Now I'm reading baby books, and they're lame."

"OK, so maybe I need to talk to your teacher about having you bumped up a grade-level or three in English. In the meantime, just get this report done the way she wants it done."

Kallan stops flopping and eyes me. "You want me to lie?"

I hold my fingers over my computer keyboard. "How about this? How about you dictate your real review, and I'll type it. That way, you get your negative thoughts out of your head, and you can better focus on the good parts of the book."

"There were no good parts," she grumbles, but she stands up and starts pacing the room, preparing her thoughts. After a few minutes, she appears at my shoulder. "Ready?"

I open a blank document. "Go."

"The name of the book is *The Trouble With Tuck the inspiring story of a dog who triumphs against all odds.*"

I stop typing to interrupt, "Is that seriously the name of the book? Or are you being sarcastic?"

"Right? That is seriously the name of the book." She points a finger. "You need a colon there."

I insert the colon and read the title aloud again. "That is a seriously lame title."

"I KNOW."

I ready my typing fingers again. "OK, let's have the review."

Kallan takes a deep breath and dictates the entirety of her review without pausing as I type. "*The Trouble With Tuck: The inspiring story of a dog who triumphs against all odds* is about a babyish girl who the book says is 13, but she acts like she is 6 or 7. The girl is named Helen, and she has this ridiculously great dog named Tuck who saves her life twice, which is just stupid. The dog goes blind, which Helen somehow doesn't notice until Tuck crashes through a screen door. How do you not know your dog isn't using his eyes anymore? Also stupid. So the vet, who starts out nice but then turns icky, says that Tuck is never going to get better and so they should think about giving him to researchers to do experiments on. That part did not seem very kid-booky ... at all ... just saying. And then Helen gets all whiny and runs away with Tuck, which does not go well. Duh. And then her mom and dad have this great idea to get Tuck a guide dog, which is not at all realistic because in the book Tuck is getting all crabby and mean and bad and is tied up in the back yard because he won't behave. If I had a dog like that, my mom and dad would so not ever get me another dog on the chance that more dogs is better. But in this book, there is a happy ending, which is also stupid. I would never recommend this book to anyone who wasn't a baby. Sincerely, Kallan."

I finish typing and look up. "I can see why your teacher might think you are not a team-player."

Kallan sighs. "OK, so how about if I dictate the exact opposite of what I want to say, and I'll turn in that version instead?"

"Hold on, let me save this version first." I click a few keys. "So the not-so-great comments you've gotten on the last few book reports ... did you hate those books too?"

"We keep reading baby books we're supposed to find inspiring." She looks at me. "I hate things people tell me are supposed to inspire me."

"So it's not really that you are doing a poor job on these reports; it's just that you are doing them your way?"

"Yup."

"I definitely need to talk to your teacher again. In the meantime, yes ... dictate the kiss-butty version of your review to turn in."

Kallan thinks for a few minutes and then she is ready.

"The Trouble With Tuck: The inspiring story of a dog who triumphs against all odds is the heart-warming story of a dog and a little girl who each save the other's life. This story will have you in tears of inspiration, and you'll be all, What the heck is wrong with my own stupid dogs who just lay around and fart and bark and do nothing at all useful never mind save my life because me personally, I own two dogs, and if the house was on fire and I was relying on my personal dogs to save me, I would have had to have thought ahead and made preparations to be trapped in the burning building while wearing an outfit of meat and dog biscuits, and then maybe ... maybe ... if the outfit was secured to my body properly, my own personal dogs would accidentally save me while trying to drag the meat-suit to safety, and if, on the way out of the building, the meat and then in turn I myself was to catch fire, my own personal dogs would eat me like they were at a BBQ but back to Tuck the dog, who is superfantabulous awesome ..."

I stop typing to say, "Really, Kallan?"

"What, too much?"

Orphan-hobo child

The girls walk into the kitchen, and Maj explains to her sister, "I have no idea why paper covers rock, I just know it means I get to hit you." She balls up her fist for the punching.

Kallan reaches to stop Maj's fist. "How many times have I told you ... you don't put your thumb inside your fingers when you make a punching fist."

"What?" Maj is defensive. "That's how I punch."

Kallan sighs sympathetically. "Listen, if you ever actually have to punch someone, you are going to break your thumbs. Show me your fighting stance ... put your fists up like you are going to fight someone."

Maj is reluctant. "I'm not planning on fighting anyone. I just want to punch you because of the game."

Kallan shakes her head. "No, this is important. Put your hands up like you are going to fight someone."

Maj balls both hands into fists, her thumbs tucked within. Kallan shrieks with laughter, and Maj huffs in annoyance. "Listen, thumbs are what separate me from the animals, and I'm not going to lose my only advantage over the dogs in a fight; my thumbs are tucked away for protection."

"But you'll break them. Tell her, Mom."

I nod. "It's true. If you're going to punch someone, thumb goes on the outside."

Maj lets her hands drop. "That makes no sense at all." She lifts her hands again and stares at her fingers and thumbs as she arranges them according to her younger sister's directions. She stares at her fists incredulously. "That can't be right! That feels insane! My thumbs are all exposed and choppable!" She shudders. "Mother, are you sure thumbs inside isn't the correct way?"

"Totally sure."

She shrugs. "That settles it, then ... I'm never punching anyone again."

Kallan feigns nonchalance. "Guess you can't punch me for covering my rock with your paper, then ... that's too ba ... OW!"

Maj stares at her fingers in satisfaction. "Good to know I've got the pinch thing correct."

"Dang it, Maj ... there is no pinching in Rock-Paper-Scissors!"

"Says who?"

Kallan rubs her pinched arm and addresses me, "Mom, I would like to take this moment to lodge a complaint against Maj."

"For pinching you?"

"What?" Kallan shakes her head. "No, no, no ... that was fair ... paper covers rock, and she's tragic at punching. No, I want to complain about the school-bus situation."

Maj instantly busies herself with the preparation of her breakfast of toast and apple slices. "Mother, there is no school-bus situation."

Kallan disagrees. "There IS, because here's the thing, Mom. You know how Maj gets to sit in the back of the bus because she's older? And I have to sit in the front because I'm younger?"

"Yes."

"OK, well the fact is that Maj is allowed to sit anywhere on the bus she likes, but she never chooses to sit with me. She always sits in the back."

Maj is busy with the complications of toast and says nothing. I try to soothe Kallan. "The thing is, babe ... I asked Maj about that, and although it would be nice of her to sit with you occasionally, I can understand why sitting in the back is important to her. She wants to feel important. She likes the perks of being one of the older kids. You'll get your turn."

Kallan waves my words aside. "No, that's not it. Listen ... I found out that every Friday, I can sit in the back. Every Friday, the younger kids are allowed to sit in the back ..."

"Really? That's terrific! Problem solved."

"No, Mom ... you interrupted me ... I'm only allowed to sit in the back if Maj invites me."

"Uh oh."

Kallan glares at her sister in frustration. "She won't invite me!"

Kallan and I turn to stare at Maj, who is stuffing toast into her mouth. She chews exaggeratedly and then swallows. "What? Just because a thing is possible doesn't mean it should be undertaken."

I sigh. "Seriously, Maj?"

"Listen, if the rule is that I am put in charge of issuing the invitation, then I am also in charge of the decision not to issue an invitation. The end. No invitation. Not from me. Not ever. I get enough of being a sister here at home. The bus is my sanctuary."

Something about Maj's phrasing catches my attention, and I ask, "**From you?**"

Maj's averted eyes tell me more than her words. "What's your point, Mother?"

I turn back to Kallan. "Does the invitation have to come from your sister?"

Kallan claps her hands happily. "Oh my gosh, is it really that simple?"

Maj collapses in pretend anguish against the countertop. "Why can't I have anything that's just mine?"

Kallan is already making plans. "Alright, so all I have to do is make friends with a few of the older girls and then drop a few hints ... maybe promise a few candy bars ..."

Maj speaks, her voice muffled against the countertop, "Don't you see how this is going to look? Don't you see that everyone is going to think it's odd that you're befriending strangers like an orphan-hobo child when your sister is standing right there?"

"Yes, Maj," Kallan agrees gleefully, "They are going to think it's strange. No way this won't be awkward for you."

Maj lifts her head and speaks pleadingly, "**AUGHGHGHHHH. MOTHER, MAKE IT STOP.**"

I walk to smooth Maj's hair. "I'm not unsympathetic, Maj, but the only one with the power to stop your sister's machinations is you."

"You mean ..." She grimaces. "You mean invite her?"

"Obviously."

Maj slumps against the counter again in despair. "I can't stand it."

Kallan dances through the kitchen behind her sister and starts making her own breakfast, the same thing she's had for breakfast the last several mornings: yogurt, orange juice, fruit, and cheese-waffles. I watch as she toasts the waffles, readies a big pile of shredded cheddar cheese, and then makes a huge unwieldy sandwich; she carefully places the sandwich in the microwave and pushes the necessary cheese-melting buttons. When the microwave dings, she removes her waffle sandwich and takes a giant oozing bite. I try not to comment, but I can't help myself. "Is there a reason to dismiss the lessons of the recent repeated past?"

"No idea what you are talking about, Mom."

Maj is horrified. "I am not going to stand here and watch her eat this again. I'm out of here." She rinses her plate and heads upstairs to brush her teeth.

"Kallan," I remind her, "Yesterday, you ate this same breakfast and then laid in the hallway, naked except for your underwear, wailing about how you couldn't go to school until 'the cheese calmed down.' That ring any bells?"

She takes another bite. "What's your point, Mom?"

"The morning before that, I seem to remember your stomach was bloated and sad as well."

"It's possible my underwear is too tight." She takes another huge bite of cheese and waffle. "Why you always gotta be dissing the cheese?"

"Whatever."

Kallan finishes her waffle sandwich happily, eats a tiny bit of yogurt and a few grapes, sips at her orange juice, throws her dishes in the sink and races upstairs to get dressed for school. She reappears twenty minutes later, her face contorted in agony. She clutches her stomach and sinks to the floor, where she curls up in the fetal position and moans, "My tummy is hard like a basketball. Mom, I think I'm dying."

"You have got to be kidding me."

"Mom, I am bloated beyond recognition. Who is this girl, you say? I don't know either, and the girl is me! I am bloated beyond recognition, I tell you. There's no way I can go to school ... they'll call the roll, and I won't know when to answer!"

"Because you don't recognize yourself."

"Mom, it hurts. My tummy hurts so bad."

Maj walks into the room and stares at her sad crumpled sister with distaste. "How many times," she asks, "does breakfast cheese have to tell you it hates you for you to get a clue?"

Kallan whimpers something that sounds an awful lot like, "If I wasn't so pleased you are going to grow up to be a serial killer, your lack of empathy would concern me."

Maj leans forward suspiciously. "What did you say?"

Kallan tucks her head against her chest and rolls about the floor like a misshapen Weeble. "I'm dying, Maj. Who knows what I might say? Also, tell Mom I can't go to school."

Maj rolls her eyes. "Of course you're going to school."

Kallan turns pathetic eyes to me. "Mom, I'm dying."

"You are not dying," I inform her, "You just need to work really hard on farting before you get to school, and then maybe you could spend a few quiet moments later in the day making plans to eat less cheese."

"But Mom, what about this moment here in which I am dying?"

"Go change into looser pants so the cheese has room to swell."

"Mom, I'm going to have to go to the bathroom about a bazillion times."

"Such is the life of a cheese glutton. If you have an accident, check with the office before calling me; I'm sure they've got some old lost-and-found sweatpants for you to wear the remainder of the day. Hold on, I'll get you a garbage bag to carry your poo-pants."

Kallan glares at me from the floor. "I am just so sure that other mothers are more sympathetic than you are."

"Want me to wheelbarrow you to some other mother's house?"

Resignedly, Kallan stands up and decides that she is perhaps not dying after all. She and her sister organize their backpacks and their lunches, and then Maj informs Kallan, "Just so you know, if you're going to be a walking cheese-fart, it might not be the best day to start introducing yourself to the other girls at the back of the bus."

Kallan whirls on her sister in anger, but then winces as a cheese-fart-to-be rumbles in her tummy. She composes herself and asks casually, "Maj, do you even know the other girls who sit in the back of the bus?"

"What? No. You know I don't like my friendships to be a function of seating arrangements. No, I ignore everyone. None of them are in my class, anyway. Why do you ask?"

Kallan considers. "So they don't know your name?"

"Obviously not."

"No reason. Just wondering."

I open the door and hold the dogs back. "OK, ladies, have a great day!"

Maj bends to tie her shoes. "I'm not quite ready, Mother. You don't have to sound so happy to get rid of us."

Kallan steps over her sister and grabs her backpack from the table by the door. She swings the backpack over her shoulder, somehow managing to bash the still-kneeling Maj in the head. Maj rises in a fury. "**WHAT IS WRONG WITH YOU? I COULD HAVE BEEN KILLED!**"

Kallan turns to her sister, her face an expression of deep concern. "Oh my gosh. Gloria, are you alright? Gloria? Speak to me, Gloria!"

Maj is confused and stops mid-rant, staring at her sister. "Gloria?"

Kallan continues in patient solicitous tones, "No, I'm not Gloria. *You're* Gloria. You hit that doorknob pretty hard. Are you alright?"

Incredulously, Maj asks, "What are you talking about?"

"Mom!!" Kallan screams, "Gloria hit her head and I think she has amnesia!"

I am still holding the dogs by their collars, and I wince. "Kallan, there is no need to scream. You are standing right in front of me."

Still speaking at top-volume, Kallan walks out onto the porch. "Gloria, come on! I'm sure your memory will return soon enough. We have to get to school."

Maj follows her sister out to the end of the short driveway, which is their bus-stop. "**MY NAME IS NOT GLORIA!**"

Kallan shifts her backpack and shrugs her shoulders as she offers explanations to the other children waiting for the bus. "My sister Gloria hit her head and she's forgotten who she is. Amnesia, it's called. You guys can help her out by calling Gloria by her name as often as you can."

The other children are scandalized and thrilled, and one boy wonders if a name-tag might be helpful. All of the children gather around a sullen Maj to appreciate the tragedy of her situation.

"**MY NAME IS NOT GLORIA!**"

"It's so sad," Kallan says, shaking her head, "Our whole family had such high hopes for her, and now look at her ... she's all ruined by a doorknob. Poor Gloria."

The bus arrives, and everyone climbs on.

Gloria yells something about cheese-farts.

Kallan yells something about amnesia and mental patients and how her delusional sister smells imaginary farts for fun ... "It's like her hobby now, poor thing."

I watch as the other children gather solicitously around Maj to escort her to a safe seat.

"GET AWAY FROM ME! MY NAME IS NOT GLORIA!"

Kallan waves happily from one of the front-seat windows as the school-bus pulls away.

Gloria glowers out of her window.

I close the door.

Turns out I'm dying

"Alrighty, this family meeting is called to order."

The girls look at me suspiciously, and Maj asks, "Since when do we have family meetings?"

"I would have merely said that we need to talk, but the last time I said we need to talk, you guys got all ridiculous and thought I was dying. No one announces fatal illness in an official family meeting, so I figured this way we could get right to the topic at hand."

"And what's the topic at hand?" Kallan asks.

"Well, girls ... turns out I'm dying."

Mark chokes on laughter and the girls glare at me. "Mother, you are not even a tiny bit funny."

I giggle. "Really? Because I crack me up."

Mark takes over. "We just wanted to take a few minutes to let you guys know where things stand and to check in with you ... see how things are going. There have been a lot of changes lately." The girls say nothing; they just stare at their father expectantly, and so he continues, "OK, well ... the first thing I wanted to tell you is that we sold the house in Vallejo. So that's done."

Kallan leans in eagerly. "Does that mean we have money to buy a house here?"

Mark shakes his head. "No, it does not. In fact, we lost money on the sale. We're fine, but we're going to be renting for a bit."

"That's a bummer." Kallan slumps back in her seat. "There's a girl in my class who has a house on the lake, and she said the house next to her is for sale."

Mark clears his throat. "Yes, well ... when we eventually buy a house again, I doubt very much we'll be in the market for a lake house. Those houses are very expensive."

"Well, that's disappointing." Kallan crosses her arms against her chest, unhappy with her family's economic status.

Maj is curious. "So when we buy a house, will we buy this house? The one we're renting?"

I shake my head. "Probably not ... but we are likely to live in this house for a few years, so you should get used to calling it home."

Kallan sighs. "Could you tell the kids in the neighborhood that? Because a few of them told me their parents said they shouldn't get too attached to me as a friend, because we're just renters, and we'll be leaving soon."

"What? Who said that? Seriously?"

"It's true, Mother," Maj says, "Also, we are apparently bringing down the property values with our renting ... that's what people have told me."

"Oh, for heaven's sake." I turn to Mark. "I swear to god, I'm just going to put a couch in the front yard and start hanging out there in my nightgown, smoking cigarettes and swearing at passersby."

Mark laughs. "It's not a big deal." He turns to the girls. "We'll just stay. You make friends and we'll stay here, and before you know it, people will forget about how they thought you were leaving, because we will have stayed. As for lowering property values ... that issue rests with the owner of this property ... not with us. The housing market is tough right now. Speaking of tough markets, that brings me to my next point, which is that I am going to be doing some contract work."

"What does that even mean, Daddy?" Maj's face is serious.

"It means that I have lined up a series of short-term jobs as I continue to look for a full-time job. It's a good thing," he explains.

"Alright," Kallan says cautiously, "Anything else?"

I step in. "Your daddy and I wanted to take this opportunity to see what you guys think of Oregon so far. We've been here a few months now ... what do you think?" The girls shrug in unison and say nothing. I stare at them. "Really? Since when are you speechless? Come on, one of you tell me something that's different here than it was in California."

Maj offers, "Big the Frog died. In California, he was always alive."

"Not quite what I was hoping for, Maj."

She tries again, "None of my old friends are here."

"Seriously, Maj?"

"What? You asked what was different. Let me think ... it rains a lot here. Like a LOT."

"I was hoping for enthusiasm," I say, but Maj ignores me and makes her next point.

"This house is not as nice as the house we had in California. Like, it's not even close. There is nothing that is better about this house than our old house."

"Maj, could you try to be maybe a tiny bit positive?"

"Let's see ...," Maj thinks, "Oh! You can't pump your own gas here! That's different."

"Not what I had in mind, babe."

"Lots of our stuff is packed in boxes."

"Try again."

"There's no play structure in our back yard."

"You are getting on my nerves, Maj."

"Oh, and there's no sales tax like there was in California! That's way different." Maj sighs. "Something else that's different? It gets dark really early here, and it's cold. And everything's muddy always."

Exasperated, I turn to Kallan. "Do you have anything to offer?"

She shakes her head. "Maj took all the things I was going to say."

I try to drag us back in the direction I intended. "I guess I was kind of hoping you would have some good things to say about Oregon." The girls seem confused, which bothers me, and so I direct them more specifically. "What about school? Isn't there anything that's different about school?"

Maj looks at me questioningly. "You mean you want us to say things like how grateful we are that you moved us to a community with such awesome schools and how excited we are that the bus comes right to our driveway to pick us up and how we are making lots of new friends and learning new things and our teachers are amazing and life is just awesome?"

I reach to tap her in the middle of her chest with my finger. "You annoy me, Maj."

"Ditto, Mother."

Kallan breaks the tension. "Oh wait! I know something that's different about the schools here! I noticed it right away."

I turn to her, "Oh yeah? What's that?"

"Everybody's white!"

Maj turns to her sister. "I know! It's weird, right? When we used to go to school, mostly there were only a couple of other kids who looked like us, and here, everyone looks like us!"

Kallan agrees eagerly, "Seriously! Even when we were home-schooling, most of our friends weren't pale like us. Everyone here is white." She settles herself to stare at Mark and me; Mark and I stare back at her, and she shifts uncomfortably. "What? I didn't say it was a good thing. I only said that it was a different thing." She continues defensively, "I'm allowed to notice if everyone everywhere I go is suddenly the same color as me."

"She's right, Mother. She's allowed to notice."

Kallan leans forward to touch my hand. "In related news? I am now officially over the whole beading-my-hair thing."

Maj rolls her eyes. "Good call, Kallan."

Mark adjourns the meeting, but not before Kallan asks, "Daddy, this contract-job thing ... is it what you want to do?"

Mark smooths her hair. "If everyone only did what they wanted to do, most things would go undone."

She tucks her body against his and looks up into his face winningly. "So shouldn't you take advantage of opportunities to do what you want to do when you can?"

He taps his chin with a thoughtful finger. "Are you thinking what I'm thinking?"

Ice cream.

Of course she is.

"MOTHER, WE HAVEN'T EATEN DINNER YET! THIS IS INSANE! DESSERT DOES NOT COME BEFORE DINNER EXCEPT IN A HOUSE OF MADNESS! HOW ARE YOU JUST STANDING NEGLIGENTLY AND USELESSLY TO THE SIDE WHILE THEY DISREGARD THE RULES OF THE UNIVERSE? ANSWER ME, WOMAN! I DEMAND AN ANSWER!"

"The answer is 72, Maj."

"What?"

"You demanded an answer. 72 is as good an answer as any, and so the answer is 72."

"Mother, someday when people ask about my childhood, **AND THEY WILL**, I am going to spill my guts everywhere."

"I look forward to the guttage."

"GUTTAGE IS NOT A WORD, MOTHER. HAVE SOME ONE-TIME HOME-SCHOOL EDUCATOR PRIDE! GUTTAGE IS NOT A WORD!"

"I assume you don't want ice cream, then?"

Maj is incredulous. "OF COURSE I WANT ICE CREAM ... THAT'S NOT THE POINT. YOU ARE SUPPOSED TO PARENT ME PAST THE INAPPROPRIATE WANTINGS. HOW DO YOU NOT KNOW THIS?"

"One scoop or two?"

"TWO, MOTHER, BUT I WANT IT NOTED I AM EATING THIS ICE CREAM UNDER DURESS AND WITH THE KNOWLEDGE A BETTER-PARENTED CHILD WOULD NOT BE EATING ICE CREAM IN THIS MOMENT."

"Duly noted."

She pauses on her way into the kitchen. "I do like it here, you know. Not everything is better, but I do like it here."

"I know, babe."

"So ask me again ... ask me what's different about Oregon, and I'll give you an answer."

"Alright. What's different about Oregon?"

"72."

It takes me a second, but then I smile. "I demanded an answer, and 72 is as good an answer as any."

Maj runs off and I listen as she joins Mark and Kallan in the kitchen. **"OK, I CAN SEE THAT SUPERVISION IS REQUIRED. MOTHER, GET IN HERE ... THEY ARE RUNNING AMOK IN THE ICE CREAM SCOOPAGE. SCOOPAGE IS NOT A WORD BUT WE ARE PLAYING FAST AND LOOSE WITH THE RULES THESE DAYS, AND SO I WILL SPEAK OF SCOOPAGE IF I DESIRE TO SPEAK OF SCOOPAGE AND WHY ARE WE ALLOWING KALLAN TO PUT SPRINKLES ON HER ICE CREAM? THAT IS JUST ASKING FOR TROUBLE, DADDY. MOTHER, I SAID GET IN HERE ... RULES ARE REQUIRED. GET IN HERE AND BONK THESE FOOLS WITH SOME RULES!"**

The best things about Oregon, I decide, are the things that haven't changed.

"GLUTTONY IS NOT AN OLYMPIC SPORT, KALLAN. I'M JUST SAYING."

Definitely.

Jazz hands

The girls are opposite sides of most coins, and so the fact they have diametrically opposed approaches to money comes as no surprise. Maj has always been frugal and conservative and Kallan has always been the exact opposite; her approach to money might best be described as giddy.

Maj saves her money, scours the racks for things that are on sale, and often talks herself out of purchases on the way to the cashier, figuring that if the item in question hasn't completely won her over by then, she doesn't really need it. As a result, Maj tends to have quite a bit of money saved up, so when she does decide to buy something, she is generally able to purchase it for herself.

If Kallan has $5.00 when she walks into a store, she leaves the store with $5.00 worth of stuff. It doesn't matter what store she happens to be in; her $5.00 is spent. Hardware store, office-supply store, grocery store ... it does not matter; if she is holding money on the way into the store, it is gone by the time we leave. Kallan is all about immediate gratification.

I never stop her. The only rule is that she may not buy candy or food (if we did not have this rule, Kallan would be a sphere). Our hope is that eventually, Kallan will learn to be more responsible with her money and to make better purchasing choices. So far, this has not happened.

The four of us have made a detour in our day to stop at a clothing store at Maj's request. Maj is not generally a girl whose head is turned by fashion or the expectations of others, but she has noticed that her California wardrobe is not helping her fit in at school. She asked around and discovered that this particular store is popular with her classmates, and so she is here to look for peer acceptance at bargain prices.

As we walk into the store, Kallan digs into her purse and comes up with exactly two pennies. Mark hands her $5.00 (her weekly allowance), and so she has a grand total of $5.02. Kallan looks sadly into her palm, in which the money rests. "Hey, Maj? How much money do you have?"

"Fifty dollars."

"Seriously?" Kallan is shocked. "How is that even possible?"

"It's called maturity," Maj tosses over her shoulder as she heads to the back of the store in search of the sales racks.

Kallan sighs, but then squares her shoulders and heads to the sparkly flip-flop display in the store's front window.

I follow Maj, because for some reason, this store has put all of the sale items far above Maj's reach. As I pull various items down from the racks for Maj's consideration, I can hear Kallan trying to convince Mark to kick in the extra $8.00 she needs to buy the $12.90 flip-flops. I try to make eye contact with Mark, because I do not want him to lend or give her money. I want Kallan to have the experience of getting nothing while her sister buys things. I want Kallan to make the connection between buying three small stuffed animals last weekend and having no money for flip-flops this weekend.

I can feel Mark weakening from across the store — they are really cute flip-flops, and it's only $8.00, and Kallan wants them so much.

Maj points to the collection of discounted dresses far above her head. "Can you get those down for me, Mother?"

As I reach for the dresses, I hear Mark explaining that Kallan can save her allowances and return to buy the flip-flops when she has the money. I sigh, because even though he is saying the right words, his tone invites discussion of how much Kallan loves her daddy and how much more she would love him if he were to help her out this one time.

"Mother, which do you like better ... the blue one or the green one?"

"I like the green one."

She hands me the green one to put back on the shelf. "OK, so definitely the blue one."

Kallan's voice rings out loud and frustrated, and it makes me smile to hear how badly she misreads her daddy in this moment. "But I don't want them in two weeks when I have saved my money! I want to buy them now! I want them now! Daddy, listen to me! I want you to buy them for me now!"

The entirety of the small store turns to see whose child would dare to speak to her father that way, and Mark puts all thoughts of his wallet away. He meets my eyes across the store, and then he marches Kallan out to the car. Kallan does not go quietly, and Maj and I pretend we are not related to her. Maj continues her shopping.

In the end, Maj buys a blue sweater dress marked down from $34.99 to $6.99 and a flowery purple blouse with flouncy layers marked down from $24.99 to $5.99. She is delighted with her purchases. She holds out her hand for the two cents back from her thirteen dollars – the no sales-tax thing delights her every time.

We walk out to the car, where we are greeted by a seething Kallan. "It's not fair! Why does she always have money and I have no money? Why does Maj get to buy things and I get to buy nothing?"

I climb into the minivan. "About that ... I want to congratulate you on leaving the store without buying anything. If you look in your purse, you'll find you have the same $5.02 you had when you walked into the store. That's called saving; your father and I wondered when you would finally grasp the concept. You're growing up! Becoming mature! We're so proud."

Kallan is furious. "Stop sarcasmming me!"

Mark smiles as he pulls the minivan out of the parking lot and we head for home. "You should focus on this moment, Kallan. Saving is a good thing. Personally, I'm feeling pretty pleased with having saved myself $8.00."

"AUGHGHHH! I saved under protest and you know it, Daddy!"

Kallan kicks at the back of Mark's seat as he drives, punctuating each kick with sour demands for money and fairness. After the fifth time I reach back to still her legs, I say mildly, "Kallan, I would just like you to know that your daddy is so much more patient than I am. If I was driving the car right now, I would be charging you a quarter a kick, and you would arrive home penniless."

Mark (who is indeed far more patient than I am) says, "Actually, that sounds like a great idea."

Kallan spends the remainder of the drive screaming and kicking herself into abject poverty.

When we arrive home, Maj models her purchases for Mark, who is properly appreciative. Kallan glowers in the background, refusing to compliment her sister. Kallan's mood does not improve when she hears what we are having for dinner: stuffed peppers. She is outraged. "Do you know how long it has been since I had a good meal?" she demands angrily as she stomps up to her room. "Why do you guys keep making things I hate?"

I call after her, "Tell you what ... stuffed peppers are the free option this evening, but there are always choices. I'll bring up a menu with various selections for dinner. You choose whatever menu option appeals to you that you can afford."

Kallan appears at the top of the stairs. "I can't pay for anything, because you guys stole all of my money!"

"That is tragic news indeed. That limits your options. Also, unless you have bail money, you need to stay in your room until I call you for dinner."

"I hate this family."

"I'll try not to let that declaration of hatred influence my preparation of your food."

"Wait, what did you say?"

I wave cheerfully. "See you at dinner!"

Later, sitting at the table, Kallan angrily stabs at her pepper. **"Why"** stab **"do"** stab **"I"** stab **"have"** stab **"to"** stab **"eat"** stab **"this"** stab **"disgusting"** vicious stab **"thing?"**

"Why do you have to complain and whine so much? Either eat a few bites and be done with it or just excuse yourself and go to bed." (That's me talking, by the way.)

"Fine." Stab stab scoop. "Watch me. Is this what you want?" She shoves a huge bite in her mouth and chews angrily. Swallows, makes a gagging sound. "I was right. It's disgusting."

I applaud and cheer and clap as though I have just been witness to some remarkable feat of circus daring. "The nice thing about serving you something that tastes so foul is that you haven't noticed the dead bugs I added to your serving."

Kallan glares at me, and I take a large bite of my own bug-free food. She takes another tiny bite of her own food. "I'm only eating another bite to prove that I know you didn't put bugs in mine."

"Awww ... it's so cute how you trust me. It's like you're new here ... all shiny *naivete*."

She takes another obstinate bite, gags a little, for real this time.

Mark turns to look at me. "She tried it. Maybe you should give her a break and not tease her."

I take another bite of my food as Kallan smirks at me and pushes her plate away. I lean across the table to address Maj instead of Mark. "You and I are the only people in this room I am enjoying right now." I put up my hand for a high-five.

Maj, who likes stuffed peppers, takes another bite of her food and stares at my palm until I let it drop. "Mother, I am not a girl of high-fiving, and certainly not while I am eating."

"Come on, Maj ... work with me. I am enjoying you. Talk to me."

She is suspicious. "You mean like small talk?"

"Yes. Exactly like small talk. I'm done with your sister and your father for the duration of this meal. It's just you and me ... bring on the small talk."

She chews silently for a moment, and then she swallows. "This afternoon, while we were shopping?"

"Yes?"

"In one of the stores we passed, there were these two store employees in the window, wrestling a mannequin out of her clothing." Maj meets my gaze. "It looked like they were attacking a small pale woman."

"Huh. I missed that."

Maj continues, "So it got me thinking ... you know what they should do?"

"What's that?"

"They should let people donate their bodies to stores after they die. And then they could use the dead people as mannequins in the windows."

I stare at her as Mark and Kallan choke back giggles. "Really? That sounds like a workable plan to you?"

She stares back at me, still thoughtful. "I know *I* would go shopping at a store that had my dead mom in the window."

I stand and start clearing dishes from the table. "Good talk, Maj."

Maj smiles, pleased, and she excuses herself from the table. She heads out into the back yard to play with the dogs.

Meanwhile, Mark is still basking in the glow of father-daughter bonding with Kallan on the subject of my sarcastic and caustic personality. As I rinse plates in the sink, I hear Mark say confidingly, "You know, Kallan ... I saw an ad in the newspaper for flip-flops at Target, and they were only $4.99. If you're willing to do a bit of apologizing, I might be willing to give you back your allowance, and then you could buy *those* flip-flops with the money you have right now. No saving required," he finishes triumphantly.

I turn to watch Kallan's reaction. She leans across the table to lay a gentle hand along Mark's cheek, and she says softly ... incredulously ... "I can have cheap Target flip-flops if I apologize?"

Mark misreads his younger daughter completely, and he nods into her caress. "Yes! Pretty cool, right?"

Kallan lets her hand fall away from his cheek, and she rolls her eyes sarcastically before bringing both of her hands up along either side of her face to shake them. "Jazz hands!" she sneers in mock amazement and celebration, and then she runs off.

Mark looks over at me. "We've ruined her. Jazz hands?"

I laugh. I laugh so hard it takes me a minute to say, "Oh my god, how did you not see that coming?"

"Says the woman who expected normal small talk and instead got a vision of her corpse as a department-store mannequin."

"*Touché*, babe."

Touché.

No bleeding required

Maj has always had issues with seasonal allergies. I had hoped she might get a break this year with the move. I imagined that perhaps her body would be so surprised by all of the new potential allergens, it would get confused while trying to process the multitude of possible problems. But Maj's body is as smart as her brain, and it has recognized all the beautiful green up here in Oregon for what it is ... an arch-enemy.

Adding to the problem is the fact that Maj has always had extremely sensitive eyes; since the age of two, she has worn very dark sunglasses whenever she goes outside. I blame myself, because when she was a baby, she used to enjoy staring directly at light-bulbs. I thought this was hilarious, and I would offer her views of bare light-bulbs all the time. Because moths are attracted to light (and because Mark and I are super clever), we took to calling her **Mothra**, after the giant killer monster moth of Japanese scary-movie fame. Secretly, we still think that's pretty funny. Maj does not.

When she went to kindergarten, she became best friends with a little girl who much much later told Maj that at first, she thought Maj was blind.

Maj gaped incredulously at her friend. "A blind girl who ran around on the playground and never bumped into anything? Didn't you wonder how I was reading and writing and walking around if I couldn't see anything?"

"But," protested her friend, "You were wearing blind-girl glasses!"

With the arrival of Oregon's spring, Maj's eyes are so sensitive at the end of the day of allergens and sunlight that even the overhead lights in our house are too much for her.

"Augh!" She turns from the brightness, squinting her swollen eyes and waving her hands in frustration and pain. "Turn the light off! It's hurting my eyes!"

"Listen, Maj, we can't just live like moles," I protest as I pour her another shot of antihistamine, "we can't live in total darkness."

"It's not total darkness. See?" She pushes a button on the remote control. "The light from the television doesn't bother my eyes at all."

When the situation worsens to the point that Maj is unwilling to go outside for any reason other than to go to school, I make her an appointment with her new doctor to get a referral to an allergist.

.....

Here we are, Maj and I, speaking to the doctor about Maj's allergies. We have spoken to a lot of doctors over the years about Maj's allergies. This conversation is just something to get through in order to get the referral to someone who can write the proper prescription, and so I nod my head and shake my head as seems appropriate; I'm not really paying that much attention. The familiar words flow over Maj and me ...

allergies, nosebleeds, photo-sensitivity, asthma, medications, steroids, allergy shots, your daughter is tiny, endocrinologist, eye-drops, allergic triggers, she's just such a tiny little thing, rinse off pollen, dust house, be aware of exposure, coughing, sneezing, endocrinologist, tiny, past medication used to control allergies, tiny, headaches, tiny, saline spray, endocrinologist ...

Wait. What? Why is she saying "tiny" so often?

I look over at Maj, who is also confused.

Endocrinologist?

The doctor prints out a nice height chart for us, and she puts a little red star at the 2% mark to represent Maj.

Maj does not care for having a crazy all-alone star represent her inadequacies where height is concerned. Maj does not care to be ambushed with a discussion of her lack of height. Maj does not care for the sound of the word 'endocrinologist.' Maj does not care for any of this, and by 'does not care for,' I mean that she seethes and boils with a white-hot fury. The doctor is oblivious, and starts talking about dwarfism. I make eye contact with Maj, which is simple, because Maj's eyes are HUGE; I shrug my shoulders in apology as I interrupt the doctor, who will not stop talking, to say, "But the most likely thing is that there is no medical issue at all, and Maj is just short, correct?"

The doctor looks Maj up and down and says, "There are over 200 different causes of dwarfism, which is defined as an adult who reaches full height at something under 4'10". Some of those causes are more serious than others. I think it would behoove you to have Maj undergo some tests."

Maj has still not said a word, and so I say, "But you don't have any way of knowing how tall Maj is going to be. She's only ten years old. Look at me ... I'm only 5'2" ... she seems like she's on track to be about my height."

The doctor looks Maj up and down again and says simply, "Not so much," and then she starts talking about a "simple" procedure used to help people gain height in which the leg bones are broken at the growth plates to encourage new bone growth. Maj and I stare at her, speechless with horror.

I take a deep breath and extend my hand. "OK, so we'll take the referral to the allergist and also the referral to the endocrinologist."

Maj somehow manages to remain silent until we get to the parking lot, and then she says, **"WHAT WAS THAT ABOUT? I AM NOT A DWARF, MOTHER. NO ONE IS BREAKING MY BONES, MOTHER. NO ONE IS BREAKING MY BONES, AND THAT IS FINAL."**

"Don't be silly. No one is breaking any bones. That's insane."

"OK, BECAUSE THAT IS FINAL. LIKE ALL THE WAY FINAL. FINAL. THERE IS NO ROOM TO NEGOTIATE ON THE BONE-BREAKING THING, BECAUSE OF THE FINALITY."

"Agreed."

"AND I AM NOT A DWARF, MOTHER."

"Of course you're not a dwarf. You know what you are, though?"

"What?"

I hold up my index finger and thumb to indicate a small amount. "You are just the tiniest bit obsessive."

"What's your point?"

"Well, now that the doctor mentioned the possibility of dwarfism ... now that she said that there may be a medical reason you are short ... are you going to be able to just put that mentioning aside and go on with your life?"

Maj sighs. "No."

"Right. So we're going to have to go see what the endocrinologist has to say, because otherwise, the worry itself is going to stunt your growth."

She kicks parking-lot gravel, resigned. "You may have a point." She huffs. "Do not tell Kallan about the bone-breaking thing, because she'll just want to build a medieval torture rack to stretch me."

"She so would." The thought makes me smile. "Please can I tell her?"

"No."

.....

And so here we are, Maj and I, in the car about a week later, on our way to the allergist for testing. Maj is also scheduled to have some blood drawn for the endocrinologist, but I may, in the interest of my own sanity, have neglected to mention that fact until now. Maj is not a fan of needles, and she has a tendency to fill the time between learning needles will be involved and the actual appearance of needles with rage against the world, with her mother standing in for the world. I turn down the radio. "So it turns out they're able to do the endocrinology testing today, while we're there for the allergist. Isn't that convenient?"

Maj is instantly alert. "What kind of testing?"

I speak soothingly, "We'll stop by the lab to have a little blood drawn, and then we'll go to the allergist."

"WE, MOTHER? WILL THEY BE POKING YOU WITH NEEDLES AS WELL?"

"I was trying to be supportive, but no ... you're right. You're the one having the tests done."

"So basically, you are taking me to the hospital to have me tortured."

"No, just blood work. It's just a single needle. They need to take a little blood."

"And then we're going to the allergy testing?"

"Yes."

"Which involves needles."

"More like pinpricks."

"PINPRICKS ARE DELIVERED BY NEEDLES, MOTHER. DON'T YOU EVEN TRY TO MAKE PINPRICKS SOUND FRIENDLY."

"Fine. There are going to be needle pinpricks and also needles for the blood draw ... it's going to be super fun."

"So basically I am going to be stabbed to death."

"Yes ... I signed the consent forms, and I remember clearly that the forms said you were going to die."

"STOP TRYING TO BE FUNNY."

"Sorry. Yes ... it's a day of needles. Allergy and endocrinologist ... both require the use of needles ... both today."

"Are you kidding me? Why did you schedule these appointments for the same day? What sort of mother does that? Do you *enjoy* seeing me poked and stabbed and punctured? Do you have some crazy needle-poking dream? You don't need a kid for that. I am happy to give you a needle and you can poke your own self."

"I do not have a crazy needle-poking dream. It's just a few tests."

"Why didn't you tell me the blood work was today?"

"Because I thought you would be upset for days instead of just an hour or so. This is easier."

"NOT EASIER FOR *ME*. I LIKE TO KNOW ABOUT THINGS. *WHY ARE YOU DOING THIS?*"

"Maj, it will be OK."

"MOTHER? I AM FINE BEING SHORT. THIS IS HOW I AM. WHY ARE YOU SO INSANE ALL OF THE SUDDEN WITH THE ... *OOOOOOOHH, I AM SO SAD. MY*

DAUGHTER IS SHORT. PLEASE HELP US! IT IS SO TRAGIC ... WHAT IS WRONG WITH YOU, MOTHER?"

"First? That is **not** how I sound. And second? I am fine with you being short. I love you at any height. The doctor just suggested that we check to be sure that there is nothing wrong. Most likely result? You are a healthy short crabby girl. And then we're done. OK?"

"What I don't understand is why no one takes my word for anything. I am telling you that this is the height I am supposed to be, **Mother**. This height. There is nothing **WRONG**. You are just all crazy needle-loving because the doctor told you to be. You need to think for yourself, **MOTHER**."

I bite my tongue, because there's no point in arguing with her ... no point in arguing that she won't be able to relax until this whole issue is behind her.

She checks the tautness of her seatbelt, finds it satisfactory. "And by the way? Newsflash, Mother! You are not a tall person. In fact, you are short. But nobody seems to care about that. Somebody needs to poke some needles in **you** and figure out what is wrong with **you**." She crosses her arms and stares angrily out the window. "Except the thing that is wrong with you is not that you are short. The thing that is wrong with you is that you like to torture your daughter."

She radiates fury for the remainder of the drive to the hospital. It's about a half-hour drive, and every few minutes I turn down the radio and ask, "Are you still angry?"

The answer is always, *"YES."*

I stop asking her after she says, *"WHAT AM I, A BABY? I AM ANGRY AND I AM GOING TO BE ANGRY FOR THE ENTIRE REST OF THE DAY. STOP ASKING ME."*

As we walk to the lab, Maj continues talking loudly about how I hate her and how I am about to have her tortured and how all of this testing is useless and how her mother just wants to see her daughter get stabbed with needles because her mother has vicious fantasies of draining her daughter's blood. Because her mother is insane. This last part, she keeps saying over and over again ...

"YOU ARE AN INSANE PERSON, MOTHER, AND INSANE PEOPLE SHOULD NOT GET TO DECIDE WHAT IS GOING TO HAPPEN TO ANOTHER PERSON. I AM TIRED OF DEALING WITH YOU BEING ALL CRAZY. THERE IS NOTHING WRONG WITH ME."

We are getting a lot of attention, but Maj doesn't notice or care because she is so caught up in her emotions.

I care ... a little bit.

Sigh.

As we wait in the lab for her number to be called, she finally runs out of steam; she sits beside me, glowering and silent and hate-filled.

I reach to brush her hair from her face. "If I didn't know how very much you love me? I would be scared of you right now. Look around ... you are scaring the people around us."

She seems pleased with this news.

We make it back to the blood-work area, and Maj climbs up into the chair. The phlebotomist comes over and casually tosses down 12 empty vials and then walks away.

Maj's eyes almost pop out of her head. **"THEY ARE FILLING *ALL* OF THOSE TUBES WITH MY BLOOD? YOU SAID IT WAS JUST A LITTLE BLOOD! THAT IS NOT A LITTLE BLOOD! MY ARM IS GOING TO GO ALL FLAT AND SQUISHY! I DO NOT HAVE THAT MUCH BLOOD TO SPARE!"**

There are more vials on the little table in front of us than I imagined there would be, and now I too am annoyed that Maj and I have been left here to consider the amount of blood that will be required to fill them.

I speak loudly to no one in particular, *"Excuse me? It does not seem like the best policy to just throw down a bunch of vials and then walk away. If someone was a little nervous about having blood drawn, this would only make the situation worse."*

And then the phlebotomist comes back and ... makes the situation worse.

She takes in Maj's furious face. She takes in Maj's size. And then she says, "Do you want to sit on your mommy's lap, sweetie?"

Maj glares at the woman and speaks loudly and clearly, **"WHAT IS *WRONG* WITH YOU? DO I LOOK LIKE I NEED TO SIT ON SOMEONE'S LAP? WHAT IS *WRONG* WITH YOU?"**

Maj turns to me. **"WHAT ... IS ... WRONG ... WITH ... HER?"**

There is no more talking then, only endless blood drawing and fury.

And then we head over to the allergist, who pokes Maj's arms with fifteen small bits of Oregon allergens. Ten on her right arm and five on the left. And then we sit and watch as most of the ten pokes on her right arm immediately begin to swell like angry mosquito bites ... a big circle of mosquito bites.

I joke that she has a big angry **O** of allergy on her arm, and that the **O** stands for Oregon. "You are allergic to Oregon, Maj!"

She is not amused.

The allergist explains that Maj is allergic to a whole host of local trees, pollen generally, mold, moss, grass, and dust.

Maj is incredulous, and she leans into the allergist's face in challenge. "Are you serious? I already knew all of that. Seriously? You brought me here to get all these pokes and big itchy bumps to find out that I am allergic to trees and grass and pollen? Why didn't you just ask me? I already knew that. Duh."

The allergist does not know how to respond to this.

I sigh and address the allergist. "Alright, so we'll just take the prescription we requested originally."

As we walk out to the car, Maj informs me, "I hope you don't think I am going to be agreeing to those allergy shots he was talking about. Because I am so *not* agreeing. One shot every week for ten months ... needles every time ... *not even*. I will just be an inside sort of girl. I don't need trees except through a window. I am not so much about being outside, anyway."

I say nothing.

She stops at the car and looks at me. "I just want to be clear. We spent two hours getting all these tests done, and the result is that I am allergic to outside stuff?"

"Yes."

"Doctors are stupid." She fastens her seatbelt. "Mother? If you think I am doing allergy shots, you should think again. I don't want to come here every week for ten months. Do *you* want to do this every week for ten months?"

Not even.

A few days later, we meet with the endocrinologist, who says, using more words than are strictly required, that Maj is short. Absolutely nothing is wrong, and in the end, Maj will grow up to be a perfectly healthy, albeit shortish, young woman. Maybe five feet tall ... maybe a bit more, he guesses.

"Another stupid doctor," Maj informs me as we leave the hospital. **"I ALREADY KNOW THAT I AM SHORT. WHY DID THEY TAKE 12 HUGE VIALS OF MY BLOOD TO COME TO THE CONCLUSION THAT I AM SHORT? I ALREADY**

KNOW THAT I AM SHORT! IF THEY COULDN'T TELL I AM SHORT, WHY DIDN'T THEY JUST ASK ME? HEY, MAJ, THEY MIGHT HAVE THOUGHT TO ASK, ARE YOU SHORT? AND I WOULD HAVE INFORMED THEM THAT YES INDEED I AM SHORT. NO BLEEDING REQUIRED." She turns and shakes two frustrated arms in the direction of the hospital and the medical profession generally. **"YOU MAKE NO SENSE!"**

We climb into the minivan, and I say, "At some level, though, you must be relieved to know there's no underlying medical explanation for your shortness."

She glances at me, surprised. "What? That was me being relieved. Just now. Weren't you listening?"

Participation trophies

We're getting ready to go out to dinner ... a casual networking event to which Mark has invited the girls and me ... an event at which he hopes to make some connections and a good impression.

The girls are determined to lower Mark's expectations.

Kallan has been provoking Maj all afternoon, and at the moment, she is torturing Maj with pretend boogers. She cups her left hand over her nose and reaches waaaaaay up with her right hand's index finger. The cupping hand shields the fact that she is not actually picking her nose, and Maj falls for it every single time.

Even though she knows she is risking big trouble, Kallan is ecstatic. "How does she fall for it *every* time, Mom? *Every time* she thinks I am putting a booger on her. It's awesome!"

Maj is hysterical, rending her garments in stiff-armed rage. "I AM SMEARED WITH NOSE LIQUID! I AM STICKIED WITH MUCUS! I AM CONTAMINATED BEYOND REPAIR! CALL 911! CALL ANIMAL CONTROL! CALL AN ASSASSIN! CALL WHOEVER IT IS YOU CALL WHEN A CHILD GOES MONSTROUSLY BAD AND MUST BE GIVEN BACK TO THE BREEDER! CALL THE FARM! I WANT HER SENT TO THE FARM WITH THE OTHER REJECTED PETS! I DEMAND SOMEONE GIVE ME THE NUMBER OF KALLAN'S BREEDER RIGHT THIS INSTANT!"

I send a giggling and unremorseful Kallan to her room; she is unconcerned. The punishment is meaningless; she knows we're headed out soon, and we won't be leaving her behind. I try to soothe Maj and reassure her that she is not covered with plague.

"MOTHER, MY VISION AND MY JUDGMENT ARE CLOUDED BY SNOT!"

Kallan doesn't even make it all the way up the stairs before she turns around and comes back. "If I apologize to Maj, can I stay down here? I'll be good. I promise."

I look at Maj, who has crumpled herself into a tiny ball at the far end of the couch. I turn back to Kallan. "Listen, stay away from your sister. I need to finish getting ready. We're running behind schedule; can you please just leave your sister alone?" I look around the room for something to keep Kallan occupied. I pull a magazine from the coffee table and hand it to Kallan. "Sit. Read. Behave yourself."

Maj looks at me, her eyes sparkling with betrayal and disbelief, and then she walks to settle herself in the window seat that looks out on the front yard. She stares sadly out at the neighborhood. She looks like one of those puppies in the pet store window that begs you with huge sad eyes to rescue it and take it home. Except no one is coming to rescue Maj. She's already home, and her home is filled with boogers.

I say hopefully, "So we're good here," as I walk upstairs to finish getting ready. Mark is already dressed, because he did not have to go yell at people about imaginary boogers.

He looks in the mirror. "I didn't shave. I shaved this morning. Do I need to shave?"

"Depends on the impression you're trying to make."

"So I should shave?"

I shrug. "Smooth or scruffy ... I think you're adorable either way."

He thinks about this. "I'd rather not shave, but what if we run into somebody important?"

I look at him. "Well, then your carefully crafted public persona is going to be trashed because you are going to be with **us**." I gesture toward the sound of screaming from the floor below. I wave my arms in frustration. "I just told Kallan to behave. I was just down there." The shrieking (all Maj; Kallan is suspiciously silent) escalates, because what is the point of shrieking if there is to be no escalation? I continue, "Babe, I think it's probably best if you just hope that we don't run into someone you're trying to impress. No one's going to notice whether you have shaved, because our daughters are going to be like a cartoon ball of fighting. That's what people are going to notice."

Mark strokes his chin, considering, and we listen together as the screaming below us reaches rabid fever pitch. He decides, "Alright here's the plan. I'll shave, just in case I run into anyone important. As for you and the girls? If I **do** see anyone I need to impress this evening, I will just grab a trophy family."

I laugh. "It is just so clear to me that you mean you would grab **any other** family and pretend to be with them." Still laughing, I walk down the stairs and into bedlam. Kallan is giggling and dancing and shrieking out protestations of innocence. Maj is literally hopping up and down, she is so enraged, screaming and screaming and screaming about how her sister put a booger on her. She pulls the shoulder of her shirt away from her body and out so that I can appreciate ... what appears to be a longish-bit of yellowy-green grossness stuck to the fabric.

I wave my hands in the air and yell for silence. "NOBODY TALK UNTIL I ASK YOU A QUESTION!"

Kallan puts one hand over her mouth and raises her other hand. Like she's in school.

"Kallan, if I let you speak, do you have words that are going to fix this situation?"

Kallan nods her head. Maj groans.

"OK, Kallan. Speak."

Kallan cocks her head at me. "OK, first? I am not a dog, Mom. Telling me to speak. Geez."

"KALLAN!"

"OK! OK! I did put that on her, but it's not a booger. See?" Kallan reaches forward and plucks the *booger* off of her sister. "It's just a strip of gluey stuff I found in the magazine you gave me." Kallan stretches the adhesive strip to demonstrate that it is not a booger. She snaps it happily in her sister's direction. In response, Maj does her best imitation of a girl whose arm is being shredded by farm equipment.

I put my hands over my ears. "Oh my god, Maj ... stop screaming ... it's glue. I see why you were confused, but it is glue."

Maj pulls back her bloody stump of hysteria and glares at me. "Mother, are you seriously reprimanding me when the mucus-felon is standing right there, snot-handed?"

I turn back to Kallan, and I extend my hand. "Give me the magazine and the glue strip, and then go up to your room. I will call you when it's time to get in the car, and if I have to talk to you again before we leave, I swear to you that I will scoop every last booger from my nose and smear them over your person."

Kallan pauses at the bottom of the stairs. "No way you would do that, Mom."

I stick my index finger right up my nose and say, "How confident are you in that assessment?"

Maj reinserts her own hand into the threshing machine, and Kallan runs shrieking up the stairs to her room. I head back upstairs as well, where I find Mark again. He asks, "Why are they both screaming now?"

I reach into the closet for a clean blouse, and I walk to the bathroom to brush my hair. "Do you really want to know?"

He shakes his head. "No. You're right. I don't." He stands before me, leans forward, and pulls his pantlegs up. "A question for you ... do these socks make me look stupid? I think the socks are too short. Do they make me look stupid?" Bent over to hike up his pantlegs from mid-calf, he looks up at me. "Well? Do they make me look stupid?"

I stare at him; his pantlegs are bunched in his hands, exposing short socks and a fair expanse of both shins. I pretend to consider his question as he holds the awkward pose. "If you wear those socks, are you going to walk around hunched over like that, holding your pants up? Because then my answer would have to be yes, those socks make you look very stupid indeed."

He laughs. "Shouldn't you get dressed?"

"I am dressed."

He pretends to consider me. "I guess I always have the trophy-family option."

I am about to protest, but our daughters come spilling into the room, an almost literal cartoon fightball, a rolling spitting ball of chaos, all pinches and hair pulls and clawed fingertips.

"MOTHER, SHE STARTED IT!"

"Well, she called me a baby!"

"AND THEN SHE HIT ME!"

"I was sitting in my room being innocent, like you told me to be, and she barged in and she pinched me!"

"I DID NOTHING, AND THEN SHE JUST ATTACKED ME!"

"I attacked her? Mom, that girl flew through the air like a tiger! Plus? Maj needs her fingernails cut."

They both press close to show me their mortal wounds and voice their complaints.

I sink to the floor as Mark heads into the closet in search of better socks. "Ladies? There has just been too much fighting lately! What is wrong with the two of you?" They stare back at me, united in their defiance. I point to Maj. "And you … why are you even upstairs? I left you downstairs, safe from the marauding mucus-felon, remember?"

Maj feigns confusion. "Mother, my room is up here. Surely you didn't mean that I, as the innocent victim, was to be refused admittance to my own bedroom."

"You guys are driving me crazy."

Maj speaks for the two of them, "This is how sisters are, Mother. If you didn't want this? You should have thought before you decided to have Kallan."

Kallan agrees, "Yeah, Mom. You should have thought. This is how we are."

"AUGH! This is not the way sisters are! Or at least, this is not the way you are supposed to be. Why can't you two keep your hands to yourselves?"

They both look at me like I am an idiot.

Maj explains, "Because she is really annoying, Mother."

Kallan nods complicity. "Yeah, she is really annoying, Mom. And so at some point? Our hands are going to be involved."

Maj agrees, "Yup."

"So despite the fact that we have discussed how you may not touch one another in anger about 8 billion times … you are both telling me that you are using your hands because your sister pissed you off?"

They both giggle at the words *pissed off*, exchange glances, and then look back at me. The word **DUH** is written all over their sister faces.

"Fine. Both of you go to your rooms, one girl per room, doors closed. We're going to be leaving a bit later than planned. Go to your rooms. Take a break from one another."

Maj is all reasonable. "Our rooms are right across the hallway from one another. This is not taking a break. This is just sending us away from you."

"Well, if that is all that can be accomplished? I will settle for that. Go. Away from me."

They turn to leave, but then Kallan pauses. "You know she's going to keep yelling at me, Mom. What am I supposed to do?"

"Ignore her."

She thinks for a minute. "So after this time in our rooms, when we go out to this dinner-thing ... if she pinches me because she is angry, what am I supposed to do?"

"Walk away."

"And if she hits me?"

"Walk away."

"And if she bites me?"

"Walk away."

"And if she bashes me with a big rock?"

"Lie quietly, as I do not wish to be disturbed."

"And if she kills me?"

"Lie quietly for a longer period of time."

She snorts. "You're funny, Mom."

"Thank you. Now go ... I told you what would happen if I had to speak to you again before we left."

From down the hall, Maj is screaming, *"DO YOU SEE WHAT HAPPENS? I GO TO MY ROOM LIKE YOU TOLD ME TO, AND SHE IS IN THERE DOING COMEDY! SHE IS SUPPOSED TO BE IN HER ROOM!"*

Kallan bows and giggles and runs to her room.

There is quiet for a moment.

Mark reappears, pulls his pantlegs up again to show me his longer socks.

I walk to look at myself in the mirror. "Babe, I was going to change, but I think this is as good as I'm going to get this evening."

He walks to stand next to me; he leans to examine his own reflection ... straightens his tie. "So are we ready to go?"

I reach to pump several squirts of lotion in my palm. "Not quite ... I have to go smear handfuls of boogers on Kallan."

He sinks into a chair, and he says, "The three of you are insane."

Like he's new here.

Innocent plagiarizing bystander

Kallan is working on her homework, and she yells out, "Mom? Is there gross food in Canada?"

"I am sure there is gross food in Canada, but I don't think they are **known** for their gross food. Why?"

"Just wondering."

She comes to find me, holds out her **Passport Book** for me to sign. She is supposed to be keeping track of how many minutes she is reading every night. At the end of each month, there is a 'Passport Party,' and the class celebrates with snacks from a different country. This month they are 'visiting' Canada. Last month they visited The Philippines, and Kallan was less than impressed with the party food. Lumpia, according to Kallan, are "nasty little rolls of disgusting."

"Although ...," I say as I sign Kallan's reading passport, "maybe they'll serve *poutine* ... it's French fries topped with little white cheese curds and a slathering of brown gravy."

She laughs. "You don't have to make up horrid things to scare me."

I meet her eyes. "No, it's true. *Poutine* ... look it up."

"Seriously?" She shudders in horror. "You know I hate gravy." Her face grows more hopeful. "I like cheese ... what are cheese curds?"

"The time I had them, they tasted like the lumps in cottage cheese, but dried off. Kind of weirdly rubbery."

"Ugh. Why can't Canada be known for its cookies?"

"Canada is also known for its maple syrup ... and bacon ... maybe you'll get lucky, and no one will think of *poutine*."

"Have you even met my teacher? No way she serves us maple syrup and bacon if gravy/cheese-lump fries is an option." She examines her reading passport and sighs heavily, wanting to be sure I know she is not pleased with my efforts. Kallan and I have been engaged in a small running battle over this passport, because I refuse to take it seriously. I am of the strong opinion that keeping track of minutes read and rewarding children who log the most reading minutes is lame and counterproductive.

As far as I am concerned, the reward for reading is the reading.

The end.

Over the years, I have opted the girls out of every reading contest that has come along. Maj, who is a reading fiend, has always agreed with me on this point. Kallan, however, is still annoyed that I refused to take her to Pizza Hut to get the multiple personal-pan pizzas she won for reading books back in 1st grade. I have no regrets; handing out small greasy pizzas as a reward for reading is so ridiculous I do not even know where to start.

Anyway. Kallan is supposed to log reading minutes. I am **not** doing this, but the form needs to be filled out somehow. We have come to an agreement: I will give her credit for 60 minutes of reading per day whether she reads or not. Some days she reads much much more, some days not at all. I do not care.

She sighs another heavy angst-laden sigh. "This is all a lie, you know. I don't read 60 minutes every night. Some days I read a lot more."

"And some days you read less. I don't care."

"Other people's parents keep track of every minute."

"Other people's parents have not given this issue enough thought, then."

"Other people's moms just follow directions."

"That explains it. I am the questioning sort."

"My teacher would like it better if you just did what she said."

"You think? I already spoke to your teacher about my feelings on logging reading minutes. You were there. You want me to call your teacher and explain it all again? I would be happy to do that."

"No," Kallan says as she hurriedly sweeps the passport into her backpack, "No need for that."

She pulls out a book-report form for me to check. I have had Kallan bumped up a few reading levels, but that has not changed the teacher's insistence that book reports be done her way. This particular book report is in the form of a pre-printed imaginary newspaper article that provides prompts for Kallan's responses about the book. I look over Kallan's efforts; she has drawn a lovely picture of her favorite scene from the book, discussed why she would recommend the book to others, provided information about the author, the title, the setting, the characters. Written a short summary of the book.

Uh oh.

I lay the paper on the table in front of me. I look at Kallan, who avoids eye contact. "Ummmmm ... Kallan?"

She continues stuffing things in her backpack, eager to be done with homework for the evening. "Yeah?"

"The book you read for this report ... could you get it for me?"

She is instantly suspicious and alert. "Why?"

"I want to look at the inside jacket."

She puts her hands on her hips. "Why?"

"Because I am thinking that when I look at the inside-jacket book summary, I will see the exact words that are written here on your paper."

Kallan stomps her foot. *"Augh. Why do you have to be all noticey? The teacher doesn't care. I promise you. She doesn't care."*

"Alrighty, then. I won't care either." I hand the form back to Kallan. "Clearly this is an issue I should be taking up with your teacher. You are just the poor innocent plagiarizing bystander."

"I have no idea how those words appeared on the page."

"It must be terrible when words turn all demonic and spew from your pencil without your knowledge."

Kallan is yelling now. *"Fine! I copied out of the book. And fine! I am not supposed to do that. And Mother? Other people's mothers are not as difficult as you are!"*

"Other people's mothers are not trying hard enough, then."

She looks at her paper sadly. "But I did a lot of work on the rest of the book-report form. I don't want to re-do the entire thing."

"Then you are going to need a really big eraser."

"But if I erase that whole section, I will lose points for being messy."

"So then you have a choice. You can redo the entire report or you can erase and take the hit for being messy."

"Can't we just let it go this one time and see if the teacher notices? I don't think she will notice."

"Nope. And if you do this again? *And I notice?* You are getting an **F**."

"You are not in charge of my grades," Kallan announces as she stares at me in challenge.

I bring my face down to her level. "Imagine me. At your school. In the hallways. In your classroom. Announcing in a loud crazy voice that you are a cheater and demanding that you get an **F**."

She stares at me, eyes flashing. "Everyone would think you were insane."

I stare back at her. "And guess what else? Everyone would know that you are a big fat lying cheater." I stand up. "Your call, babe."

She sighs. "Where is the eraser?"

I turn to my computer and type a short email. Kallan looks up from her erasing to watch me hit *send*. "Wait, did you just send an email to my teacher?"

"Yup."

"About my book report? But you said I could erase and rewrite it!"

"No, I just mentioned how very much you were looking forward to sampling the foods of Canada."

Kallan's eyes widen. "Let me see that email. The word ***poutine*** better not be in that email."

I open the email and Kallan reads aloud. When she gets to the part where I mention how very much I think the class would enjoy the Canadian delicacy *poutine*, she turns on me. "What is wrong with you?"

I read the email I sent aloud again, softly, and I feign great astonishment. "I have no idea how those words got there."

"Very funny, Mom."

"It must be the demonic word-spewage thing you mentioned earlier. How could I have doubted you?"

"Gravy, though ... on French fries? That's like a nightmare!"

"Don't forget the lumps."

"What?"

"Don't forget your cheese lumps ... one always has to take one's lumps." When she looks confused, I explain, "The phrase *take one's lumps* means that one must suffer the consequences of one's actions."

Kallan rolls her eyes. "Have I mentioned lately how pleased I am to have escaped your home-schooling clutches?"

"So in this case, the lumps are of the cheese-curd variety, but they are also a metaphor for the consequences of your cheating."

"I GET IT, MOM."

"Do you, though?"

She ticks off the main points on her fingers. "Plagiarizing is bad." (one finger) "Personal integrity is good." (two fingers) "Blah blah blah ..." (three, four, and five fingers, which she then balls in a fist she waves in my general direction)

I stare at her. "Your parents must be very proud."

"Indeed they are."

Drop your sister off somewhere

I am driving the girls to the library, and the subject of birthdays comes up. Maj will be eleven soon.

Maj is several years away from driving, but she likes to torture her sister when she can. As we drive, Maj announces, "Kallan, I'm going to be sixteen a whole two years before you. For two whole years, I will be able to drive a car while you'll be doing what you always do."

Kallan looks up from her cellphone. "What's that?"

"*Not driving a car.* Duh."

Despite her sister's rudeness, Kallan is actually pretty excited at the thought of her sister driving her places. "Maj, when you get your license, you could drive me to the movies! Or to my friends' houses! Or to the park! That will be so cool!"

Maj curls her lip (I don't see this, because I am driving, but I can hear the curl of her lip in her next words): "I *so* don't think so. What would be the point of having a driver's license if I am not able to drive away from ... you?"

I glance in the rear-view mirror in time to see Maj making little brushing-away movements with her fingertips in the direction of her sister.

"Mommy! Maj is being mean!"

I glare into the reflection. "Yes, well ... what Maj might be forgetting is that she won't be able to buy a car when she is 16. She'll be using Mommy's and Daddy's cars. And when you want to use someone else's car, that person sometimes lets you use the car only if you run an errand for them."

Maj's face grows suspicious. "What kind of errand?"

"Like stopping at the grocery store for bread. Or getting the car washed. Or ... like dropping your sister off somewhere."

Kallan breaks in, her voice concerned, "SOMEWHERE?? You're going to have to be more specific than that or Maj is just going to drop me off *somewhere* on the side of the road."

"Good one!" I laugh.

"No, I'm serious, Mom. Make sure you tell her *exactly* where to drop me off."

"That seems like a bad deal for me," grumbles Maj.

"Plus, Mom will probably make you pick me up, too! That will be excellent!" Kallan crows.

Maj is quiet for a moment and then asks, "How much would my own car cost, anyway?"

"Way more than your allowance, Maj, and even if you get your own car," Kallan informs her as we climb out of the minivan at the library, "it might turn out you need me anyway."

"And why is that?"

"Well, if you don't get any taller than you are now, you're going to need someone else to work the pedals." Kallan runs giggling ahead of her slightly shorter older sister and through the library doors.

"Mother!! Can't you *do* something about her? I demand that you crush her." Maj blocks my path and tries to wilt me with an angry stare.

I step around her and ignore the glare. "I just don't see why you couldn't have been excited about driving and also have been nice to your sister. Would it have killed you to agree to drive your sister to her friend's house ... *five years from now?*"

"I don't want to drive her anywhere."

"Well, babe," I say as I put my hand on top of her head and steer her toward the library, "then I hope you don't need your sister to work the pedals."

When we get back home, Mark listens to the tale of the driving discussion, which turns into a discussion of the rules of the road, which turns into a discussion of bicycling. I hear Mark agree to supervise the two girls as they practice riding their bikes up and down the small street in front of our house. Before moving here, Maj and Kallan had never ridden their bicycles on a regular road; they had always ridden in parks and on hiking paths. Remembering my single bicycling outing to the park with the girls, I am delighted to sit this one out. I settle myself on the couch with a library book as the three of them head off.

They are gone for about 15 minutes, and then Maj is back. She comes stomping into the house and throws her helmet in the closet. "Daddy's yelling at me about how I have to stop bossing Kallan, but he's letting Kallan ride on the big street, and she is not allowed to do that!"

"OK, but between you and Dad, who would be the one in charge of Kallan?"

"That is not the point! Daddy is letting Kallan be dangerous! Someone needs to speak up! And then he just yells at me. Plus," she adds over her shoulder as she goes in search of a snack, "Kallan tried to run me off the road, and Daddy didn't even do anything."

I don't get the chance to respond, because Kallan stomps up the driveway, angry and shouting and red-faced; right behind her is Mark, who is also angry. He takes Kallan by the shoulders and steers her toward the stairs. "You need to go up to your room and stay there for a while."

I reach to take Kallan's helmet from Mark's hand. "Geez, what happened?"

He is exasperated. "She wanted to go out onto the big road, and I let her go on the big road for a minute, but then she wouldn't come back."

Maj gives me a *See? What did I tell you?* look from behind her father.

Mark continues, "She started screaming at me about how I wasn't listening to her, and she wouldn't listen to me, and she kept screaming, and then she just tossed her bicycle in the road and threw herself into the ivy." He looks at me, still frustrated. "She just lay there screaming in the ivy, her bike in the road. She looked like she had been hit by a car." He runs his hand through his hair. "So I couldn't just walk away like I wanted to, because I couldn't just leave her crying in the ivy on the side of the road. I knew the next car was going to stop to check on the poor injured girl, and then I was going to look like an idiot."

As Mark is talking, Kallan is still screaming about her cruel father from her room, and Maj is *I told you so-ing* with her eyes.

And then with her voice; she turns to her father and says sassily, "I *told* you not to let her go on the big road."

So Mark sends Maj to *her* room as well, and then we listen as the girls continue to loudly argue.

Mark sinks into the couch. "What is *wrong* with them? I try to do something nice, and they're both just nuts."

"Just think," I say as I sink down next to him, "How much fun you're going to have teaching them how to drive."

Mark smiles at the thought, "No, I'll only have to teach Maj." He snorts with laughter, "and then Maj can teach Kallan."

"NOT IN A MILLION YEARS WILL I TEACH THAT CHILD-BEAST TO DRIVE, MOTHER. NOT IN A MILLION YEARS!"

Kallan is determined to have the last word. "Fine by me, because I would prefer if the person teaching me to drive didn't have to sit in a booster seat to see through the front windshield."

"WHEN I DO GET MY LICENSE, I AM GOING TO RUN HER DOWN. MARK MY WORDS, SHE IS GOING TO BE ROADKILL. OK, DON'T MARK MY WORDS BECAUSE THERE'S NO POINT IN RECORDING EVIDENCE AGAINST ME AT THIS POINT IN TIME SO SCRATCH THOSE WORDS AND MARK MY INTENT INSTEAD NO DON'T MARK MY INTENT BECAUSE THAT ALSO MAKES ME LOOK GUILTY MARK MY PROPHECY THAT KALLAN WILL BE RUN OVER IN MYSTERIOUS CIRCUMSTANCES SHORTLY AFTER MY SIXTEENTH BIRTHDAY PURELY BY COINCIDENCE YES, JOT THAT DOWN SOMEWHERE ... THAT WILL DO."

Kallan asks in a casual too-loud voice, "Hey, Maj ... what's the date today?"

Maj answers without thinking but then thinks. "Why?"

"No reason. Just thought that if you are going to die today, you'd like to know the date. You know, for your records."

"AIIIEIEEEEEE! MOTHER, KALLAN IS THREATENING MY LIFE WITH VIOLENCE AND DOOM AND TAKING ADVANTAGE OF MY DESIRE TO HAVE ADVANCE NOTICE OF CHANGES IN MY LIFE."

"Death is the biggest change there is," Kallan informs her sister politely, "so you are very welcome for the notice."

"MOTHER, I AM IN JEOPARDY. ACCORDING TO MY NOTES AND SCHEDULES, I AM IN IMMEDIATE JEOPARDY!"

Kallan is solicitous. "Not immediate jeopardy, Maj. Shall we say three o'clock? Yes, let me pencil in your murder for three o'clock. That will give you time to organize your defensive maneuvers and also prepare to meet the sister-reaper."

"AIIAIIEIEEEEEEEEEE!"

Mark leans his head against the back of the couch and closes his eyes. "Did she say three o'clock? That gives me time for a nap."

Bone to pick

I bought one of those whole roasted chickens from Costco. Mark is not a big fan of dealing with chicken bones, so I am cutting the meat from the chicken and bagging it for later use. Kallan watches as I cut.

"Hey, Mom?" she asks, "Can I have the wishbone? I want to make a wish."

"Yeah, if I don't break it. Chicken wishbones are pretty small."

Kallan rests her chin on the counter next to me and watches as I work. "Do *I* have a wishbone?"

"Sort of. It's not exactly the same shape, and we don't call it a wishbone, but it would be right there." I point with a gloved hand to the spot right below her throat where her bones meet beneath the skin.

She pokes about in her chest. "Here?"

"Hold on." I remove my grease-coated rubber gloves. "Right here."

She giggles and pulls away as I touch her. "That tickles!"

I pull out another pair of latex gloves. Maj comes into the kitchen just as I am pulling them on. She stares at me for a second or two and announces, "I'm not going to be able to eat that chicken after seeing this."

I survey the chicken carcass. "Really? Well, maybe you are going to be a vegetarian when you grow up. Meat has bones, babe."

"No, I don't mean that. I mean I am not going to be able to eat the chicken because you are touching it with dog-poo gloves."

In addition to the occasional roasted chicken, we buy latex medical gloves in bulk from Costco, and I use them for all sorts of things. Dog poo clean-up is one of them. Messy food preparation is another. Toilet cleaning is another, but I decide not to share that piece of information in this moment. I wiggle my gloved hands in Maj's direction. "It's not like I used these *very* gloves to pick up dog poo." I turn my attention back to the chicken. "And even if I *were* to ever re-use the gloves I use for dog-poo duty, it's not like I wouldn't rinse them off first."

I hold up a handful of chicken for her inspection. "See? I don't see a speck of poo. You can't prove these gloves ever touched poo."

She rolls her eyes. "Whatever. I just know I am not eating poo-rubbed chicken meat."

I clap my gloved hands as I exclaim, "How did you know what I was making for dinner? Poo-rubbed chicken meat! It's going to be delicious!"

Kallan comes back into the kitchen and asks for chips. I agree. She pours two small piles into napkins and hands a share to her sister. Chomping her chips noisily, Kallan watches as I start cleaning up. "*Chomp chomp chomp* ... did you find the wishbone?"

I hand it to her.

"It's tiny! Can I still make a wish on it?"

"Sure, I guess ... maybe a smaller wish."

"*Chomp chomp chomp* ... hey, Mom ... when you die?"

I sweep the last bits of trash into the garbage. "Mmmm hmmmm?"

"*Chomp chomp chomp* ... can I have your wishbone?"

I hear her question, but she has caught me off guard, and so I say, "What?"

"*Chomp chomp chomp* ... when you die, can I have your wishbone?"

I shake my head. *"NOT EVEN."*

"Why? You won't need it anymore."

"Wherever I am, and whatever happens to me next? I am taking my wishbone with me."

"*Chomp chomp chomp* ... that seems kind of selfish."

"Really? Not wanting you to snap my dead bones so that you can wish for a candy bar seems selfish to you?"

"You don't know I was going to wish for a candy bar."

"So what was your wish going to be?"

Kallan ignores me and turns instead to Maj, who is licking the salt off of her chips before eating them. Maj knows I hate when she does this. Kallan is cheerful. "Hey, Maj! Can I have your wishbone if you die?"

Maj considers as she licks salt. "Depends. Would you use it to wish me back to life?"

"What? Don't be silly. No."

"Then you can't have it."

Kallan sneaks up behind her sister and reaches around her neck, pretending to cut her sister's wishbone out with the sharp edge of a chip. "Pleeeeeeeeaaaase??? It's just a little bone."

Maj screams as though she is actually being attacked and cut open, **"MOTHER!!! THE MANIAC IS TRYING TO KILL ME!!! SHE'S TRYING TO CUT ME OPEN AND STEAL MY BONES!!!"**

I am giggling, Kallan is giggling, and Maj is pissed.

"YOU DON'T CARE THAT SHE IS TRYING TO KILL ME? ARE YOU INSANE??"

"Honestly, it does seem the quickest way to put an end to your horrific chip licking," I point out.

Kallan quickly shoves the chip weapon in her mouth. "*Chomp chomp chomp* ... all I did was touch her with my finger. I did not chip-threaten her!" She swallows and then picks up another chip. "And even if I did, it's not like I was going to really hurt her." She runs the edge of a chip across her own forehead and then across her own neck as well. "Look at me! I am killing myself! AIIAIIAIAIAIIIEEEEEEE! I am stabbing myself to death with a chip!"

Maj storms off as I laugh hysterically.

Kallan throws herself to the ground at my feet and dies a dramatic death. In the midst of her death throes, she crumbles the chip onto the front of her shirt, and both dogs hurry over to pay their respects to the dead.

She reaches up and feels the Labrador's chest as the smaller dog licks salt from her face. "Do dogs have wishbones?"

Ugh.

Thought-o-graph

One of Kallan's baby teeth fell out this morning. It has been spectacularly loose for several days, but I have not been allowed to do more than marvel from afar at the horror of it. Every time I tried to look more closely, she would shriek and run the other way. And then, from across the room, she would demonstrate how she could push it with her tongue so that the tooth pointed forward and out of her mouth. Maj was of the opinion Kallan should be required to keep her mouth closed until the goreshow ended, and whenever Kallan poked the tooth out in Maj's direction, Maj voiced her opinion thusly:

"MOTHER, ALL I WANT IS FOR KALLAN TO BE LOCKED IN THE BASEMENT FURNACE ROOM. ALL I WANT IS TO NOT HAVE TO SEE HER BODY AS IT REJECTS PIECES AND SPITS THEM ABOUT THE HOUSE IN A BLOODY MESS. MAYBE WE COULD GET HER MOUTH WIRED SHUT ... IS THAT A THING? PLEASE TELL ME THAT'S A THING, BECAUSE I HAVE SAVED A LOT OF ALLOWANCES, AND I AM WILLING TO KICK IN MY FAIR SHARE OF WIRING THIS CHILD SHUT UNTIL SHE SWALLOWS THE TOOTH. IT WOULD SERVE HER RIGHT IF SHE HAD TO POO IT OUT ... DO YOU HEAR ME, KALLAN ... I SAID THAT I AM GOING TO HIRE SOMEONE TO HOLD YOU CAPTIVE IN THE BASEMENT AND WIRE YOUR MOUTH SHUT UNTIL YOU SWALLOW THE LOOSE TOOTH AND POO IT OUT I GUESS THE POO-SIFTING WILL BE AN EXTRA CHARGE ... WHAT? THIS *IS* ME BEING REASONABLE

AND LOVING ... GET YOUR TOOTH AWAY FROM ME! AIAIIEIEIEIEIEIEEEEE!"

It's been a long few days.

Finally, this morning, the adult tooth underneath got tired of wearing a baby-tooth hat. It gave a mighty adult-tooth heave, and a small shiny baby tooth was suddenly tumbling free in Kallan's mouth. As Kallan sits on the counter beside the bathroom sink, I hand her a cup of water. "Here. Rinse."

As she rinses and spits bloody water everywhere, she reads dollar signs in the tea-leaves of carnage. "I'm finally going to be able to buy those sparkly flip-flops!"

Kallan is still obsessed with the sparkly flip-flops she didn't get to purchase a few weeks ago. Not so obsessed that she has managed to save her money to buy the flip-flops, but still ... every time she looks down at her gym-shoe clad and decidedly unsparkling feet, there is outrage. She did try to save her money; she got as far as $10.00, just three dollars shy of the sparkly flip-flops' $13.00 purchase price, but then tragedy struck a few days ago when we happened to wander through a gift store: she bought a $9.99 miniature notebook encased in a tiny silver jeweled case.

She came to me the evening of the purchase with a sad face and the tiny notebook in hand, her voice mournful. "Why didn't you tell me not to buy this?"

"Oh, sweetie, I tried to tell you it wasn't a good idea, but you get to make your own purchases and spend your own money, and this is what you chose."

She pouted out her lower lip. "But now I don't have any money."

"Yes, that's how it works. If you spend your money, you no longer have it for other things."

"But it's just paper and a pen in a silver box. I thought it would be more fun, but it's *boring*."

"Sorry about that."

Her eyebrows lifted hopefully. "Is there any chance you want to buy it from me so that I have money again?"

"Nope, no chance. I do not need a tiny silver notebook."

She went to talk to her father, who was in rare form. "What you have there is a thought-o-graph," he told her.

"A what?" She looked at her purchase doubtfully, hoping that perhaps she had missed something.

"A thought-o-graph, in which you can record your thoughts and dreams. You'll have them forever! Written down in teeny tiny letters. Such an excellent purchase."

"Mom! Daddy's being sarcastic again!"

I looked up from my computer. "That's why I love him, babe."

She sank to the floor between Mark and me, opening and closing the little silver notebook. *Snap. Snap. Snap.* She looked up at us. "I don't suppose there's any chance that you guys would just buy me the flip-flops because you love me so much?"

I laughed and patted her head. "We do love you, soooo much, but we're not buying you the sparkly shoes."

"Hmmmmmmph." Kallan tossed the notebook on the ground in front of her. "*Hmmmmmmph.* I wish I hadn't bought this dumb thing. Now I don't have any money and I will **never** get those shoes. And by the time I **do** have money, they won't have the shoes anymore."

Mark stopped typing and interrupted her sulking. "I have a great idea!"

"What?"

"Why don't you take out your notebook and write yourself a little note about how you shouldn't buy dumb things the next time you have money? That's exactly the sort of thing a thought-o-graph is designed to record."

As Kallan stared angrily at Mark, I suggested, "You should also write in there about how you need to remember to fix your bed in the morning." I high-fived Mark over her cranky head. "See, Kallan? You bought something wonderful! A thought-o-graph, in which you can remind yourself to do things differently next time. Plus, you can keep track of chores!"

She ran angrily screaming from the room and I called after her, "I will never have to tell you to put your clothes away again! Make a note, Kallan! Make a note!"

Back to this moment, and Kallan spitting the last traces of blood from her mouth.

She speaks gleefully in between spits, "Once the Tooth Fairy comes, I will have plenty of money for the sparkly flip-flops!"

I hand her a towel. "Kallan, the Tooth Fairy isn't going to bring you $13.00 for sparkly shoes."

"Why not? She knows I need $13.00."

"Yeah, but the Tooth Fairy generally brings $3.00 or $4.00, maybe $5.00 for a really troublesome tooth. Not $13.00."

Her face clouds over with anger and the certainty she is about to be cheated. "But one time Maj got $25.00 for a tooth. I remember! One time she got $25.00 from the Tooth Fairy."

"Yes, I remember that too."

Kallan crosses her arms in challenge against her chest. "So why won't the Tooth Fairy bring *me* $25.00?"

I cross my own arms and stare back at her. "Hmmmmm. Let's think. Because *this* tooth didn't come out when your sister pushed you down and smashed your face into the kitchen tile floor, that's why."

She wilts. "Oh yeah. I forgot about that part."

I tap my lips with my forefinger. "As I recall, you were upset your sister wouldn't share her candy with you."

"I said I remember," Kallan says grumpily.

"Yes, I definitely remember that you wrestled your sister to the ground because you had already eaten your candy, and you wanted Maj's candy as well. That was a proud parenting moment." I reach to wipe an imaginary tear of pride. "Sometimes being your mother is so awesome, it's difficult to explain to medical professionals without sounding insane."

"Hush up, Mom."

"So yes ... the Tooth Fairy was extra-generous to Maj when she learned that the tooth she was picking up had been knocked out in a fit of sister-raging candy-greed."

"I feel like you are occasionally a bit grudgeful, Mom."

"I'm not holding a grudge. I'm just explaining that the Tooth Fairy views dental assault and mayhem with a different eye than she does ... say ... a desire for sparkly sandals."

Kallan leans forward to check her altered smile in the mirror's reflection. She lowers herself off of the bathroom counter and heads off glumly, tooth in hand. "I am never going to have enough money for those shoes. Never."

From the closet, where Mark is getting dressed for work, comes a voice. "Hey, Kallan!"

Mark cannot see Kallan's face, but I can ... written across her features is absolute delighted certainty that Daddy is going to solve her twin shortages of money and sparkle. "What?"

"The way you're feeling right now? Go write it down!! Where's your thought-o-graph? This is a job for the thought-o-graph!"

There is an instant in which the meaning of his words doesn't register, but then I watch as her hope dissolves into a scowl. "You guys just don't want me to sparkle. You're trying to keep me down ... make me plain."

I laugh. "Yeah, your father and I have a detailed scheme by which we plan to keep you average."

Mark emerges from the closet and smiles at Kallan. "So far, our scheme is failing miserably."

Kallan sighs, holds up the tiny tooth to the light. "About being normal ... Mom, you may have to go talk to my teacher again."

"Seriously? What is it this time?"

"We were discussing hypothetical questions in class, and she asked for examples."

"Uh huh ..."

Kallan shrugs. "So I raised my hand and said that I was wondering, hypothetically, if my mother's dead body would fit in the big lidded garbage cans we have here in Lake Oswego, and if it would fit, whether the garbage men would notice anything unusual during pick-up."

"You wondered if you would be able to dispose of my dead body in our garbage can?"

She raises her hands, palms defensive, as Mark snorts with laughter. "Hypothetically speaking, Mom."

I rub my eyes; it's too early to be this tired. "I look forward to hearing from your teacher."

Kallan nods. "We decided ..." She pauses and explains, "Even though my teacher wasn't happy about it, mine was the only hypothetical question the class wanted to talk about, so we decided ... the crows would spoil the secret. Whenever anyone puts something crow-delicious in the garbage, a huge swarm of crows shows up early in the morning before the garbage truck, all screaming and flapping their big unsecret wings. The crows work together to flip open the lid and eat whatever awesomeness is inside." She meets my eyes. "You've seen them, Mom. The crows throw everything everywhere. Pieces of your body would be up and down the street."

I stare at her silently. Mark is still laughing helplessly. Kallan puts up defensive palms again. "That's what the class decided, Mom. That part wasn't my fault. The crows and the body parts up and down the street ... none of that was me. I was just the original curious girl."

"The original curious girl who wondered about stealthy disposal of her mother's dead body ... why am I dead anyway? Have you murdered me in this hypothetical scenario?"

Kallan is suddenly newly fascinated with her baby tooth, and she rolls it in her palm, studying it carefully. "Ummm ... the thing about hypothetical questions is that you're not supposed to get all bogged down in details, my teacher said."

Mark collapses laughing into a chair, removes his glasses, wipes tears from his eyes. "Oh my god ... as though we could keep you plain."

I sigh. "Let's move on. Kallan, go put your tooth somewhere safe so you remember to put it under your pillow for the Tooth Fairy."

She doesn't move. Instead, she asks Mark, "What's it called when you make someone pay you in exchange for a promise that you won't do something?"

"Extortion?"

She shakes her head. "No, that sounds bad. Isn't there another word for earning money by promising not to do things to people?"

Mark thinks for a minute. "So you're planning on asking for protection money?"

"Yes! That sounds much better! How does that work?"

I interrupt, "You better not be thinking of asking me for protection money in exchange for the promise not to stuff my murdered body in a garbage can."

Kallan ignores me, and Mark asks her, "What exactly are you talking about *not* doing?"

Kallan is wary. "Hypothetically speaking?"

Mark agrees. "Hypothetically speaking."

She holds out her tooth in an extended palm. "I was just thinking that maybe I could make a little sparkle money promising not to chase Maj around the house with my tooth." She runs off before either Mark or I can voice opinion about this plan, and then we listen as she puts it into immediate effect. Or rather ... we listen to the sister who Kallan hopes will pay to be protected:

"I KNOW YOU ARE KIDDING ME RIGHT NOW, KALLAN. NOT ONLY WILL I NOT PAY A DOLLAR IN EXCHANGE FOR THE PROMISE THAT YOU WON'T BITE ME WITH YOUR DISCONNECTED TOOTH, I WILL IN FACT POUND OTHER TEETH OUT OF YOUR HEAD IF YOU THREATEN ME AGAIN. MOTHER, GET DOWN HERE AND PARENT THIS CHILD INTO SUBMISSION!

WHAT?

Of course her body would fit in the garbage can."

Like the big pig that you are

Mt. Hood is a bright white mountainous background presence as we go about our daily business here in Oregon, and the girls have been staring longingly at its brilliant glistening snowiness. A Saturday arrives on which there is absolutely nothing planned, and as much as I would like to just sit on the couch and enjoy the nothingness, I drain my coffee cup and ask Mark, "You feel like taking a drive up to the snow?" Mark is agreeable, and so I head into the kitchen to start packing sandwiches and bottled water.

The dogs settle at my feet in case I am inclined to throw them sandwich meat. This never happens, but they are ever-hopeful. I make Kallan's sandwich: ham, mayo, mustard, and a generous messy handful of shredded cheddar cheese. I cut the sandwich into triangles and slide it into a sandwich baggie. A couple of cookies, a few carrot sticks, some chips ... Kallan's all set. I pack similar lunches for Mark and me, with the addition of tomato slices and lettuce and minus the cheese shreddings.

I move to make Maj's sandwich. She just likes turkey and a slice of Swiss cheese. No condiments. Easy. Except we appear to be out of Swiss cheese. Unsure whether the Swiss cheese is a deal-breaker, and knowing we have other options, I hold off on packing Maj's lunch. Instead, I start gathering scarves and boots and mittens and winter coats. Somewhere in the garage, we have a couple of red plastic sleds; Mark goes off in search of the sleds as I contemplate bringing a dog with us.

As I contemplate, Jack the terrier runs to find me so that he can barf on my feet. He literally ducks his head low and tracks me as I try to sidestep the horror; he is determined to deposit the mess on my bare toes. I leap onto the couch and tuck my feet beneath me as he spews up a colorful mess. When he finishes spasming, I lean down to inspect the pile, which is a garish mixture of dog food and rainbow-colored rubbery remnants. "Where did you get balloons, Jack?" He whirls and runs away from me, up the stairs and into another carpeted room, where I can hear him barfing again. I call up after him, "Alright, so that makes this decision simple: you're staying home, vomit-dog."

Kallan comes bouncing downstairs. She points behind her. "Pretty sure Jack is barfing in your bedroom."

I walk to get paper towels and carpet cleaner. "I know. He ate balloons."

"What did you mean when you said he's staying home? Where are you going? If I promise not to throw up, can I come?"

"We're going to drive up to Mt. Hood."

"YAY!" Without moving, Kallan turns and screams at the top of her lungs to her sister, who has not yet come downstairs, "HEY, MAJ! WE'RE GOING TO DRIVE TO THE SNOW! YAYAYAYAYAYAYAYAYAYAYAYYY! WAKE UP, MAJ! WE'RE GOING TO THE SNOW!"

Maj appears a few minutes later, bleary and sullen, and she stares at me as I scrub at the carpeted barf-balloon stain. She sniffs. "Gross, Mother. I can smell loosed fluids. This is not how I want to start my day."

"Seriously, Maj?" I look up at her. "I think of the two of us, I'm the one who gets to complain."

"What's this about going to the snow? You know I hate surprises. You didn't say anything about this plan yesterday."

"Sorry about that." I stand up and gather the carpet-cleaning supplies. "I'll be back down in a minute ... I think Jack made another mess upstairs."

She stares at me. "So we understand one another?"

"Yes. You're unhappy. We're going to drive to Mt. Hood. Oh, and we need to pack you a lunch."

Kallan appears, her lunch bag in hand. "Thank you for packing my lunch, Mom! Can I put in an extra cookie? Say yes, because I already did ... a few times."

I laugh. "Yes."

Maj glowers at me. "So we *don't* understand one another."

"What is there to understand, babe?"

"I don't want to go to the snow today."

"Yeah, I got that ... we're going, anyway. You'll have fun once we get there ... promise. Also, as long as we are discussing how proud I am of your ability to go with the flow, we're out of Swiss cheese."

She yells right into my face, *"YOU ATE ALL OF THE SWISS CHEESE, MOTHER? OH, THAT'S JUST GREAT. ALL I NEED IS ONE SLICE OF CHEESE FOR A SANDWICH, BUT NOOOOO. YOU HAVE TO EAT ALL OF THE CHEESE."*

"Maj, everybody ate the Swiss cheese, including you. Don't be silly."

She glares at me. **"YOU ATE IT ALL, MOTHER. YOU JUST SIT HERE AT HOME ALL DAY WHILE WE'RE AT SCHOOL, AND YOU DO NOTHING BUT EAT CHEESE."** She stomps off into the kitchen, and I stand, carpet-cleaning supplies still in hand, trying to decide between addressing the mess upstairs or addressing the mess of Maj. Mark walks into the house from the garage, and Maj screams out, *"GET IN HERE, MOTHER! YOU NEED TO PACK ME A LUNCH! ARE YOU*

KIDDING ME? YOU HAVEN'T EVEN STARTED YET! PACK ME A LUNCH!" Mark looks at me, eyebrows raised questioningly, and I shrug my shoulders.

Maj mess it is.

I walk into the kitchen. "OK, so you need to go back up to your room and start the day over again. You are being ridiculous."

She refuses. **"I DO NOT HAVE TIME TO GO TO MY ROOM, MOTHER. I NEED TO GET READY TO COOPERATE IN PLANS THAT HAVE BEEN FOISTED UPON ME. ALL I WANT IS A DAY OF RELAXATION, BUT NO ... THAT IS TOO MUCH TO ASK. MUST BE NICE TO LAY AROUND ALL DAY DURING THE WEEK AND EAT CHEESE WHILE I'M OFF AT SCHOOL BEING A PRODUCTIVE MEMBER OF SOCIETY. SO NO ... I WILL NOT BE GOING TO MY ROOM, BECAUSE I DO NOT HAVE TIME FOR YOUR DEMANDS."**

"Guess what, Maj? You *do* have time to go to your room, it turns out. You *must* have time. Because talking to me that rudely? Always means that you are sent to your room. You know that."

She stomps off. **"WEEKENDS ARE SUPPOSED TO BE FUN! WHAT IS WRONG WITH YOU? YOU ARE STARTING MY WEEKEND OFF ON A VERY SOUR NOTE INDEED."**

During her absence, I clean up after Jack, who did indeed balloon-barf in our bedroom. I wash my hands, and turn to the matter of Maj's lunch; I discover we have strawberry jelly. I make Maj a peanut butter and jelly sandwich. I am about to wrap up her sandwich when Maj reappears. **"I AM OUT OF MY ROOM WHETHER YOU LIKE IT OR NOT, AND I DON'T WANT PEANUT BUTTER AND JELLY."**

"Don't care. Eat it or don't. I am not discussing your lunch with you anymore. Could you please try to cheer up?"

"This is as cheerful as I get, Mother. Deal with it." She walks over to see what else I have packed in her lunch. "Only two cookies? Are you kidding me? I want another cookie."

"Nope."

"Why not? There are lots of cookies. Why can't I have another one?"

I turn to her. "Because you are being spectacularly unpleasant, and anyway ... I need to save the rest of the cookies, because when you go to school on Monday, I am going to cover them with melted cheese and eat them all. Yup ... that's my Monday-plan, pretty much. Eating melted cheese and cookies."

"Might as well. It's not like you do anything else around here."

I take a deep breath. "It is lucky for you I am mostly mature, Maj. Because the immature part of me whose feelings are getting hurt? That part of me almost just licked your sandwich." I finish bagging her sandwich and packing her food. "But because I am mature? Your lunch is completely unlicked." I extend the bag in Maj's direction. "You're very welcome."

She grabs the bag. "Mother, you are so disgusting."

I ignore her insult. "Maj, take a look at the snow-clothes I put on the couch; make sure everything you need is in that pile."

Maj walks into the living room, and after a minute, she calls out, "Which scarf is mine?"

"The blue one."

"No way I'm wearing that ugly blue scarf."

"Oh my god, Maj ... trade it for another scarf. I don't care. I am not emotionally invested in you wearing the blue scarf."

"Fine, Mother."

"Fine."

"Oh, and eat some breakfast, Maj ... we want to be on the road in a half hour or so."

"WHY MUST YOU PLAGUE ME LIKE A DEMON, MOTHER?"

"OK, so back to your room you go."

"I DO NOT HAVE TIME FOR THIS NONSENSE!"

"Except turns out you do."

"AUGHHHHHH."

.....

It's a beautiful drive – not quite 90 minutes from our driveway to the snow-park parking lot. Kallan spends the drive chattering about the changing scenery and how she plans to make Persie pull her sled. Persie the Labrador sleeps through the drive, happy to be included, oblivious to the plans to make her a sled-dog. Maj stares out the window and refuses to engage, although she perks up a little bit when the world turns white, and I hear her whisper, "I didn't know there would be this much snow."

As we pull into the snow-park's seemingly unplowed lot and park the car, I say cheerfully, "You ladies should probably get changed into your snow-gear." There is the immediate sound of Kallan's seatbelt unbuckling, and she starts burrowing through the piles of coats and boots for her items.

Maj is aghast. **"WE'RE SUPPOSED TO CHANGE IN THE CAR?"**

I turn around in my seat to look at her. "Why is that a problem, exactly?"

"MOTHER, I HAVE TO TAKE THESE JEANS OFF AND PUT ON THE LEGGINGS THAT GO UNDER MY SNOW-PANTS. ARE YOU SERIOUSLY SUGGESTING I JUST GET NAKED IN THE MINIVAN? THAT IS INSANE!"

"The back windows of the minivan are tinted, Maj," I reassure her. "Unless someone is standing right next to the front of the car, there's no way for anyone to see anything at all. Besides, how long is your butt going to be out ... a second ... maybe two?"

"THE LENGTH OF THE NUDITY DOES NOT MATTER IF IT IS OBSERVED, MOTHER. DON'T YOU KNOW ABOUT PAPARAZZI? A CLICK'S WORTH OF NUDITY, THAT'S ALL THEY NEED."

"Luckily for you, you are crazily unfamous. I doubt the paparazzi have followed us, Maj. Anyway, aren't you wearing underwear?"

"UNDERWEAR IS THE NUDITY OF THE CLOTHING WORLD, MOTHER."

Kallan snickers as she pulls off her own jeans and pulls on her leggings. "Maj, get dressed. You are holding us up. I want to play in the snow." Kallan turns to me excitedly. "Mom, how deep is the snow here in the parking lot, you think?"

I open my door, just a bit, to look down at the snow, and Maj freaks out. **"I KNOW YOU ARE KIDDING ME RIGHT NOW, MOTHER. I AM NAKED! I AM NAKED AND YOU ARE OPENING THE CAR DOOR TO INVITE PASSERSBY TO THE SHOW. MAYBE YOU WANT TO SELL TICKETS, MOTHER! STEP RIGHT UP AND SEE SOME BUTT! WHY ARE YOU ALWAYS SO INSANE?"**

Mark lowers his window and reaches his open palm out into the falling snow as if to accept cash. "STEP RIGHT UP TO SEE THE NAKED KETTLE CALL THE POT BLACK! Two dollars to see my daughter's screaming naked butt."

Kallan shrieks with laughter. "That sounds like her naked butt is doing the screaming."

"THIS FAMILY DRIVES ME INSANE! HOW DO I BELONG TO YOU? WHERE IS MY REAL FAMILY? I DEMAND YOU PRODUCE MY REAL FAMILY!"

I pat at the air around Maj as though that might soothe her. "Sweetie, get dressed and we'll stop by the bathrooms and then we'll go sledding."

She pauses in the middle of pulling on her snowpants, her teeth clenched in anger. "Let me get this straight. We're all going to get bundled up in layers and layers of winter clothes, and then before we do a single thing in the snow, we're all going to take off those layers of clothing to go to the bathroom?"

I turn to Mark and he nods, and I say to Maj, "Your father and I both drank coffee on the way. We have to pee."

Kallan nods. "Me too. I have to pee."

"WHY ARE WE GETTING DRESSED TO GET UNDRESSED?"

Kallan is curious. "I only have to pull my pants down ... do you really take off all your clothes to go potty?"

"NO, YOU FOOL. I WAS MAKING A POINT. ALSO, WHY DOES EVERYONE IN THIS FAMILY HAVE TO PEE ALL THE TIME? I DON'T NEED TO PEE. NO ONE REASONABLE HAS TO PEE AS MUCH AS YOU PEOPLE. PRETTY SURE MY REAL FAMILY DOESN'T PEE THIS MUCH. YOU ARE GETTING IN THE WAY OF MY ENJOYMENT OF THE DAY."

I mumble as I pull on my mittens and grab the dog's leash, "Yeah, because the rest of us are the ones messing with the day's joy."

"WHAT DID YOU SAY, MOTHER?"

"I said I am super impressed with your bladder skills, babe. Come on ... let's go."

"Where's my scarf, Mother?" She starts digging in the seat pockets, as though the scarf might have snake-wandered about the car and secreted itself in a crevice.

"No clue. Which scarf did you bring?"

"Me? I didn't bring a scarf."

"Oh, I misunderstood ... your scarf is the blue one, then."

"Mother, there's no blue scarf back here."

"Think back, Maj ... back at the house, when you were screaming about how you wouldn't wear the blue scarf ... any chance you did something with the blue scarf that causes it not to be in the car with us?"

"I threw it in the closet."

"That explains its absence. So did you get yourself another scarf?"

"Why would I do that? I'm not the mother around here."

Mark speaks reasonably, "No, you're not the mother. You're the girl without a scarf."

"I'll just use your scarf, Mother."

"Nope. I need my scarf."

"Daddy?"

Mark turns to consider Maj, and he says, "Just zip the hood onto your coat and tighten it around your face. That's as good as a scarf any day."

"DADDY, I CANNOT BE SEEN IN PUBLIC WITH A HOOD ZIP-ATTACHED TO MY COAT. I NEED TO WEAR MY KNITTED HAT AND NO ZIPPED HOOD ... WITH A SCARF. HOW IS THIS COMPLICATED? HOW ARE YOU PEOPLE SO COMPLETELY UNABLE TO MEET MY

NEEDS?"

Mark opens his door and climbs out of the minivan. Kallan follows suit. I get out as well, and I take Persie with me. I grab the handle of the minivan's sliding door. "Maj, you stay here while we go to the bathroom. You stay here and try to find a path to reason and politeness. We'll be right back." I pull the automatic door's handle, and it starts sliding shut. Maj throws herself into the back of the minivan, screaming and rolling and hissing with frustration and fury; Mark and Kallan and I stand there for a moment as the door seals shut, awestruck by the ferocity of her emotions, and then ... all at once, we start to giggle.

"I HEAR YOU AND I HATE YOU. I HATE YOU ALL. I HOPE YOU PEE INTO YOUR MITTENS LIKE THE IMBECILES YOU ARE!"

Still giggling, we head over to the port-a-potty bathrooms and all three of us manage to pee without spoiling our mittens. Persie pees as well, although not in the port-a-potty; she turns to inspect the yellow snow. "Good girl, Persie." We walk back to the minivan, in which Maj still fumes. I sigh. "You guys go ahead. I'll hang out with Maj until she calms down." They head off, and I open the car to grab my lunch ... more specifically, my sandwich. "Hey, Maj? I'm just going to stand outside the minivan until you get yourself under control. No hurry. Not like you're being unreasonable or anything."

It's too early for lunch, but eating the sandwich accomplishes two things: it gives me something to do while Maj flings herself noisily about the car, and it empties out a baggie for Persie poo collection. Somehow, I forgot to grab the doggy-bags on our way out of the house.

The minivan is literally rocking back and forth with Maj's emotional tumbling, and because we scored the parking spot closest to the entrance of the park, I get a lot of weird looks from passersby. As the van rocks and Maj's screams carry out over the snow, a group of men and women assemble right at the park's entrance, and it soon becomes apparent they are practicing to be search and rescue workers on Mt. Hood. They gather in a circle not 10 feet from me, and their leader begins to lecture about safety on the mountain. The lecture is interrupted and punctuated by Maj's screaming, and eyes slide my way as I stand nonchalantly beside the minivan with my dog, eating a sandwich as my kidnap victim shrieks and pleads for rescue.

By this point, Maj has left all reason behind. Most of her words are garbled into incoherency by emotion, but a few hateful hissing things float clear as a bell over the snow:

"WHY WOULD YOU CHOOSE TO BE SOMEONE'S MOTHER IF YOU WERE PLANNING ON TREATING HER THIS WAY?"

"YOU'RE EATING YOUR SANDWICH NOW? WHAT'S WRONG WITH YOU? IT'S NOT LUNCHTIME — LATER, YOU'LL BE HUNGRY AND YOU'LL JUST STEAL ALL OF OUR SANDWICHES LIKE THE BIG PIG THAT YOU ARE!"

"YOU'RE MEAN AND EVIL! YOU CAN'T HOLD ME CAPTIVE IN THE CAR LIKE A PRISONER!"

"YOU CAN'T TREAT ME LIKE A SLAVE! I'M COMING OUT! I AM OPENING UP THIS SLIDING DOOR!"

There is audible giggling from the would-be rescuers as tiny beautiful Maj steps out of the car all haughty and angry to demand that I hurry up and take her to where her sister is sledding. I don't think any of them can quite believe all of that anger and rage and volume was coming from such a small adorable person. I look down at Maj as she testily pokes one mittened hand into my stomach to get me to move. "Not yet," I say as casually as I can manage, holding up the last bits of my sandwich, "I want to finish my sandwich first."

"MOTHER," she says, with hatred and evil dripping from her tongue, **"IT'S CALLED WALKING *AND* EATING. *AT THE SAME TIME.* YOU SHOULD TRY IT SOMETIME. IT'S *AMAZING.*"**

As casually as I can manage, and struggling to keep a straight face, I reach behind her to re-open the minivan's sliding door. "Back in the car, Maj. You are not ready to join the rest of us yet."

After another ten minutes she runs out of steam and emerges again, quieter and calmer. She apologizes, we talk, she apologizes again, and then she runs off with her sled as though nothing has happened. I stare after her as she runs happily away, and then I look down at the dog. "You ready, Persie? Kallan wants you to be a sled-dog."

Not quite. First we have to use that sandwich bag.

Sometimes she just explodes (Maj, I mean ... not Persie).

Poo logs with gravy

Dinner at our house.

Mark has made Salisbury steak, because 1) he grew up in Michigan and is craving Midwestern gravy-covered delights, and 2) he figures the girls like hamburger, so they will like Salisbury steak. On the second point, he could not have been more wrong.

The girls have been happily playing with friends, oblivious to dinner preparations. The friends go home, and we call the girls to the table; Kallan walks through the kitchen and spies the food Mark is arranging on a platter. She stops short and brings her hand to her mouth as if to hold back vomit and makes small barfing sounds in her throat. "Bleaaagggghhh, ohhhhhhhhh, blaaaaeeeghagh ... what *is* that?"

Mark ladles the gravy into a bowl as she watches in horror. "It's just hamburger, gravy, and potatoes. You'll like it, you'll see."

Kallan clutches at her stomach and steps closer to survey the food. "It does *not* look like hamburger. Ewwwwww. Do you want to know what it looks like?"

I walk into the kitchen and grab Kallan by the shoulders, spin her around and direct her toward the dining room. "*No,* Kallan. Go sit down."

Kallan greets Maj at the table and sits down. "Did you *see* it, Maj? It looks like logs of poo with loose poo poured over the top. Did you *see* it?"

So then Kallan is sent to her room for a little bit. Returns. Apologizes sulkily.

Dinner is served. Each girl gets a very small helping. Both girls look pleadingly up at me as though I have, in fact, served them a plate of poo logs with loose poo poured over the top.

But I am not in a generous mood. I stare at them with my best bossy-mom glare. "I want you to eat the food I have put on your plate. Even if you don't like it, I want you to eat it politely. I am sick of all this nonsense."

Kallan pokes at her food with her fork. "I've read a lot of books in which there is a bad cafeteria lady who serves *mystery meat*," she says as she drags gravy-trails across her plate, "I'm pretty sure this is what they are talking about." She traces an unhappy-face of gravy and grumbles, "Mystery solved."

Maj is deeply unhappy, but she can see that I am not in the mood for compromise, and so she says, "Can I borrow a solution from the dogs?"

I assume she means she is going to wolf it down without pausing to taste it, but then a thought occurs to me. "If you are asking if you can feed it to the dogs, the answer is no."

Maj shakes her head. "No." She picks up a tiny bit of food and puts it in her mouth; she throws her head back several times in a row; and then, staring up at the ceiling, she vigorously massages her throat to coax the food down.

I am puzzled. "OK, first? Gross. And second ... how is that borrowed from the dogs?"

"This is how you make the dogs swallow pills or medicine they don't want to take." She repeats the entire process, this time adding dramatic gagging sounds at the massage-and-swallow portion of the show. Mark, who is sitting next to Maj, pretends not to see her, but from where Kallan and I are sitting, it is quite a spectacle.

Kallan freaks out. "She is making me barf! Make her stop!" She leans across the table to yell at Maj, "That is so gross, Maj! Stop rubbing the food down!"

I press my fingers to my temples as I let my head fall forward into my palms. It's been a long day. Without looking up, I say, "Maj, stop rubbing the food down. It's gross. Kallan, stare across the table at your daddy instead of at Maj. I'll pay attention to Maj; you just mind your own business."

"Yeah," says Mark, "watch me."

I glare at Maj, who puts down her fork and glares back at me.

Beside me, Kallan holds one hand up to shield herself from the sight of her sister, and she stares intently across the table at her daddy. I take a sip of orange juice and watch Mark as well; he takes a bite, throws his head back, and then pretends to gag it down, rubbing his throat to help it along. For an instant I am furious, but only for an instant, and then fury becomes helpless laughter. I laugh and snort and try to swallow the orange juice, but I fail, and I spit orange juice across the table and into Maj's general direction. Germ-phobic Maj starts screaming and shrieking about contamination, and I cannot stop laughing. Mark swallows and makes exaggerated sounds of culinary joy, and I completely lose it. Maj cranks her shriek-volume as high as it will go, and all is chaos.

When order is restored, Kallan's plate is empty. She took advantage of the pandemonium to eat her food in big rude chomping bites. "It wasn't that bad," she reports as she scoops herself some applesauce, "Kind of like hamburger."

Maj stares sadly at her own plate, where the loose-poo gravy is congealing over the poo log. She takes a tiny bite. "Seems like I should get to decide how much yuck I want to eat."

"Not today. Eat up." I am still giggling, which annoys Maj.

"Seems like you have the phrase backwards, Mother. *My* pain is not supposed to be *your* gain."

"Good one, Maj! Now eat your dinner."

She struggles through and finally manages to finish while Kallan dances gleefully in the background. "I'm already finished ... la la la la la la la ... I'm finished," she sings tauntingly.

We start clearing the table. I glance down and notice Jack the badly behaved terrier grooming himself maniacally, which he only does when he has just ... "KALLAN!!!!"

Her face pops around the corner. "Yes?"

"Get in here! Did you feed your food to the dog?"

"No."

Kallan is an exceptional liar, and if I wasn't staring at the dog cleaning what I'm certain is gravy from his furry face, I would believe her. "Listen, I am going to ask you one more time. I am just too tired for any more of this. And before you speak, I want you to imagine leftover Salisbury steak for breakfast. With syrup poured over it. Got that image? Hold it. Savor it ... **Now talk.**" I wave my finger in her face, "And I will be smelling a certain dog's breath when you are done talking."

She stares intently into my face, gauging the seriousness of my threat. She caves. "OK, fine, I fed it to the dog. But he was happy to eat it! You guys were all giggling and screaming, and I *really* didn't want to eat it and Jack *really did* want to eat it."

She looks down in submissiveness but not apology. "So I threw it all on the floor and made pretend chews when you looked."

Maj is *outraged.*

"ARE YOU KIDDING ME? MAKE HER SIT DOWN AND EAT THE LEFTOVERS! PUT HER TO BED! TAKE AWAY HER CELLPHONE! LOCK HER IN THE LAUNDRY ROOM! DO SOMETHING! DO SOMETHING! DO SOMETHING!"

I inform Kallan that she is my slave for the evening, and that her slave duties start with emptying and then refilling the dishwasher. She stomps off. Maj is not impressed. "ARE YOU KIDDING ME? I ATE THE NASTY BARFY FOOD AND SHE DIDN'T EAT ANY? THAT IS NOT FAIR! SHE LIED! SHE LIED! SHE LIED! I WANT HER TO EAT THE LEFTOVERS! I WANT HER TO EAT THE LEFTOVERS! MAKE HER EAT THE LEFTOVERS!"

From the kitchen comes the sound of the garbage disposal as Kallan rinses the serving plate.

"*Those* leftovers?" she asks sweetly.

Pine snacks

Kallan struggles with her bicycle helmet, and once she gets it snapped, she lifts her face high and awkward to tell me, "Mom, I am totally a wilderness survivor. If I ever get lost in the wilderness, I would be fine. I know how to take care of myself. I am filled with competence."

"Your helmet is on backwards."

She unsnaps it and takes it off to examine it. "Is that what was wrong? I wondered why I couldn't see."

"You were saying something about being filled with competence?"

She rights her helmet. "I need you to tell Maj to stop being all superior about the fact that she went to Outdoor School. She keeps telling me she knows how to survive in the wilderness. She keeps saying that I would die."

Maj has recently returned from a week-long camping trip with her entire grade from school, and although she has kept the details mostly to herself, she has taken every opportunity since returning to inform Kallan she will die in the wilderness.

Maj arrives on the scene. "Well, she would die, Mother. It's a fact. She has none of the specialized knowledge I have, and she would die."

"Mom, make her stop being so annoying."

"Pointing out a small child's vulnerabilities is not annoying, Mother. I am merely stating facts."

"All your specialized knowledge is going to be worthless when I kill you and eat you."

"MOTHER, DID YOU HEAR WHAT SHE JUST SAID? SHE THREATENED TO TURN ME INTO BEEF JERKY."

I lift Kallan's bicycle out of the minivan, and I turn to address Maj. "I'm sure your sister just meant that because she has none of your specialized knowledge, she would be unable to hunt or effectively forage for food, and there you would be ... all juicy and delicious looking."

"HOW EXACTLY ARE YOU HELPING THE SITUATION, MOTHER?"

Kallan mimes swinging a big rock. "I don't need special training to turn you into food, Maj. Just a willingness to chew through the tough parts."

"MOTHER, ARE YOU SERIOUSLY GOING TO LET HER CHARADE MY BRAIN-BASHING?"

I swing Maj's bicycle out of the car. "Listen, ladies. I can see no reason either of you would ever be lost in the wilderness, so can we just agree that you would each be doomed? Independent problem-solving is not a particular strength for either one of you."

Maj takes her bicycle from me and kicks at the kickstand. She kicks at it again. And again. She growls in frustration and gives it a final impotent kick before flinging the bicycle down into the dirt. "This bike is broken, Mother. Where's a dumpster?"

Kallan considers her angry sister and the dead bicycle. "You're kind of making Mom's point, Maj."

"You're one to talk," Maj points out. "You're the girl who was wearing her bicycle helmet as a face-mask."

Kallan cringes. "You saw that?"

I pick up Maj's bicycle and roll it a few feet so the pedal moves out of the way of the kickstand, which then cooperatively folds up and out of the way. I hand the bicycle back to Maj. "Where is your father, anyway?"

Both girls point and Kallan says, "He's back there talking on his phone like we don't belong to him. You know how he does." Both sisters stare at their father as he talks happily in the distance to a possibly imaginary person on the other end of the line whose incredibly important needs are keeping him from participating in his family's unpleasantries. I take out my own phone and dial his number. I watch as he startles and then switches over to the other line.

He turns to look at us, but he makes no move to walk in our direction. "Yes?"

"Hey. Kris here. I bet you are curious about why you are standing in a park, right? Just reminding you that you agreed to walk with me while Maj and Kallan ride their bicycles. Hang up on your girlfriend and let's get going."

The girls giggle wildly as he says a few more words to whoever is on the other line and then walks to where we are. Falsely cheerful, he says, "Looks like we're all set!" He looks at them more closely. "What on earth are you two eating?"

I'd forgotten that Maj **has** shared one bit of survival advice, advice Mark hasn't yet heard. Kallan holds out a branch. "Pine needles! Maj told me that she learned at camp that if you are ever lost in the wilderness, you can eat pine needles!"

Maj shakes her head. "Not the old ones ... just the fresh bright green baby ones."

Kallan tosses a few more needles in her mouth. "Mmmm ... minty! I love these! Who knew you could eat stuff that grows on trees?"

"Besides everyone in the world who has ever eaten an apple, you mean?" Maj nibbles a few more needles and straightens her helmet. "You ready to ride?"

Kallan grabs another pine branch. "Let me just grab some pine snacks for the road."

Mark turns to me. "They're eating pine trees?"

"On the upside, their breath has never been fresher."

Mark and I walk along the path. The girls disappear ahead of us on their bicycles, but the path meanders through the park and back to where we started; there's no way for them to get lost. Mark reaches for my hand, and I laugh. "Enjoy the moment while you can; there will be a raving lunatic girl between us before you know it." We walk for a few steps; the park is lovely and green and quiet.

And then there is the far-off sound of screaming. The screaming approaches us. Because it belongs to us. Of course it does.

And then there is a girl between us. Screaming. A raving lunatic. All piney fresh. It is Maj, and she is furious and outraged and covered in dirt and sticks.

"KALLAN HURLED ME INTO THE BUSHES! I COULD HAVE BEEN KILLED! SHE CRASHED INTO ME AND THEN SHE JUST HURLED ME INTO THE BUSHES AND THE PRICKERS!"

I have a mental image of Kallan lifting Maj above her head and tossing her into the brambles. I fight back giggles. "She *hurled* you?"

"YES, MOTHER! SHE *HURLED* ME! I AM PROBABLY COVERED IN POISON IVY AND POISON OAK AND YOU DON'T EVEN CARE! SHE IS HORRIBLE! PUNISH HER!"

I stoop to brush off the worst of the dirt and plant-life that is clinging to Maj, and Mark asks, "So you just left your bicycle back there on the path? Why didn't you pick it up and ride back to tell on your sister?"

Maj turns to him and speaks slowly, as though he is perhaps a small and stupid child, **"I LEFT MY BIKE BECAUSE KALLAN HURLED ME INTO THE POISON IVY. I COULD HAVE BEEN KILLED. WHY ARE YOU WORRIED ABOUT THE BIKE?"**

I sigh. "Tell me again about your specialized survival skills, Maj."

"I ... COULD ... HAVE ... BEEN ... KILLED."

We walk together to where the tragedy occurred. Kallan does not ride back to meet us, and is in fact riding in lazy innocent circles when we arrive. She waves at us as she makes another loop. "Hi! Just so you know? Maj fell."

Maj's bike is lying in the thick weeds and blackberries that line the path. Both of its wheels' spokes are choked with vegetation, suggesting a fair amount of speed when she left the road. The whole area around the bike is trampled down, and if I was able to read the emotion of the scene, I would say there is much rage here.

Maj gestures angrily. **"DO YOU SEE? SHE COULD HAVE KILLED ME! I AM PROBABLY COVERED IN POISON. SHE TRIED TO POISON ME!"**

"Maj, there is no poison here. You fell and you are dirty, but you are not poisoned."

"SHE COULD HAVE POISONED ME. I COULD HAVE FALLEN INTO A PIT OF POISON IVY AND BEEN KILLED!"

"Yes, she could have thrown you into a pit of metal spikes, too. But she did not. You are going to live, unpoisoned."

Mark helps Maj clear the bike's wheels of green, and I head over to talk to Kallan, who is still making lazy innocent loops on her bicycle. "Kallan?"

She stops in front of me, as adorable as she can be. "Yes?"

"You want to tell me what happened here?"

"It's a small path, Mom. It's skinny."

"Go on."

"There's not much room for passing."

"Uh huh."

"So I was trying to pass her, but her bike is bigger and it goes faster, so I was trying to race past her."

"So far so good."

"And then she was calling me a baby. She called me a baby on a baby bike."

"Mmmm hmmm."

"And so I passed her and then she fell."

"Seems like maybe you skipped something there."

"Maybe I called her *shortie*."

"Something else."

"Maybe I called her *midget on a clown bike*."

"Something else."

Kallan looks at me. "OK, I pushed her over. It was a tiny push, and she was all slowed down to name-call at that moment, so she only crashed a little. But then she got all dramatic and crazy and stomped around dragging her bicycle in the weeds screaming about poison."

"OK, so apologize, and then you will be walking your bike for a while."

"Oh, man! Seriously?"

"Seriously."

Maj grudgingly accepts the apology, and then, satisfied her sister is being punished, rides ahead, all pride-injured and stiff.

Kallan walks with us. In between. A raving lunatic of unrepentance. I quickly grow tired of her, and so her punishment is short-lived. We send her on her way, and within a few short minutes, we can hear Maj's screams of incredulity that her sister is riding again so soon after trying to poison her.

Mark takes my hand. "Our children are insane."

"Seriously."

"OH MY GOSH DEMON OF VENOM AND SISTER-JERKY HOW DARE YOU RIDE YOUR TREADS THROUGH THE POISON AND THEN THREATEN TO TIRE-TRACK ME LIKE A SKUNK. I AM GOING TO TELL ON YOU SO HARD YOUR HEAD WILL SPIN AND FALL RIGHT INTO A PIT OF SNAKE VIPERS NO I DON'T HAVE SNAKE VIPERS THIS IS HYPERBOLE YOU FOOL. AIIEIEIEIEIEIEE ... GET YOUR TREADS OF DOOM AWAY FROM ME!"

Mark stops walking, and still holding my hand, he gestures at the lush mossy wilderness that surrounds us. "I like it here, lunatic children aside. Here in Oregon, I mean. This move has been good. We're doing alright here."

"Yes. Yes, we are."

Crushed beneath ponies

"Alright, here's what I have noticed." Maj picks up her fork and examines it carefully. "I have noticed that when we go out to eat here in Oregon, we always go to a brewpub."

Mark sips at his beer. "What's your point?"

"There are other restaurants, Daddy."

"Huh." Mark takes another sip of his beer. "Do these other restaurants make their own beer?"

I raise my glass to his. "Good one, babe."

"I just want to know why we always have to go to brewpubs," Maj persists, "Kallan and I don't get a say."

Kallan looks up from her menu, shakes her head. "Leave me out of this, Maj. Brewpubs have grilled-cheese sandwiches and tater tots, and I have zero complaints."

Maj is annoyed. "Kallan, why can't you ever be on my side?"

In response, Kallan turns to her sister, "Hey, Maj? How about you tell me the last time you were on *my* side, and then I will consider joining your brewpub protest."

Maj thinks for a moment. "The problem, Kallan, is that you are always wrong. If you were ever correct, it would be simpler for me to point to a long history of supporting you." She taps an index finger to her chin. "So I don't think your point is relevant here — which should come as no surprise — because I would have to be completely lacking in good judgment to be on your side. You should try being more like me," she finishes helpfully, "smarter and better able to properly make reasoned decisions."

Kallan glares at her sister for a second, and then she turns back to Mark. "I like brewpubs, Daddy. Let's agree to always eat at brewpubs."

Mark raises his glass to toast her suggestion. "Fine by me. That's why we moved here."

Maj is instantly incensed. **"DID YOU JUST SAY WE MOVED HERE FOR THE BEER?"**

I choke on my own drink. "I'm sure that's not what your daddy meant."

Mark considers and then doubles down as he raises his glass for another sip. "Good schools are a bonus, though ... I'll give you that."

Maj is aghast. **"I DO NOT FIND YOU AMUSING, DADDY."**

"I have a question," Kallan announces, "Why do all the brewpubs up here in Oregon serve tater tots?"

"They were invented here."

"Really, Daddy? " Kallan is delighted. "Is that true?"

"Well, maybe *invented* is the wrong word. Once upon a time, people at Ore-Ida had a huge pile of leftover potato scraps from making their other potato products, and they said to themselves, *I wonder if we could shape this garbage potato crap into balls and sell them?* Turned out they could, and then someone named the resulting deep-fried potato balls *tots* and an empire was born."

"An empire?" Maj is doubtful.

Mark leans forward to stare into Maj's eyes. "You've never heard of the Tottoman Empire? What exactly are they teaching you at that school of yours?"

"MOTHER, CONTROL YOUR MAN. HE IS DRUNK AND SPEAKING FALSELY OF EMPIRES."

"Drunk?" Mark protests, "I've had less than half a glass of beer."

"I guess I know drunk when I see it."

Instead of rising to the bait, Mark turns his menu around to indicate an offering to Maj. "They have a chicken-breast sandwich that looks like it might be good."

Maj does not look up from her own menu. "Like I'm going to be taking dining advice from a drunk person."

I am about to intervene, but Mark doesn't miss a beat. He puts down his menu and stares across the table at Maj for a second before turning to Kallan, who is seated beside him. He looks back at Maj, his eyebrows knitted in concern. "When did Kallan's head get so much bigger than yours? Maj, your head is all out of proportion. It's tiny! That's so weird."

Maj is stunned. **"WHAT DID YOU SAY?"**

He turns from one daughter to the other. Kallan leans obligingly across the table to offer a side-by-side comparison. Mark looks at the girls' heads assessingly for another second or two, and then he reaches for Maj's hand comfortingly. "It's not so bad. Little heads are nice."

Enraged, Maj turns on me instead of her father. **"STOP LAUGHING, MOTHER. THE DESTRUCTION OF YOUR OLDER DAUGHTER'S SELF ESTEEM IS NOT A PROPER SUBJECT OF AMUSEMENT."**

I am saved from having to respond by the arrival of the waitress and the taking of food orders. After the waitress walks away, Kallan changes the subject. "I want a pony."

I laugh. "We've discussed this before. If you imagine being able to measure the distance between you and owning a pony, you know where your pony is standing?"

"Where?"

"On the moon."

Kallan throws herself back in her seat. "Hmmmph. When I grow up? I am going to have a mansion. A mansion made of diamonds and glass and wood ... and there will be a whole floor for ponies. It will be twenty stories high, and one whole floor will be for ponies."

I smile. "And will we get to visit you in this mansion of ponies?"

"Nope. You and Daddy are the people who have made my childhood so sad and pony-less. I will have servants to keep you out."

Maj protests, "Hey! I am not keeping you from having ponies! Why can't I visit?"

Kallan considers, "I am thinking that Maj may live in the barn outside of the mansion. The ponies will not need the barn. Maj can live in the barn."

I laugh. "That's sweet that you imagine your sister living with you."

Kallan protests, "Not *with* me. She'll be outside in the barn. Duh. Every time I leave my mansion, I will drive by the barn and Maj will be all beggy like a homeless person on the side of the road, and I will give her nothing except perhaps a bag of pony poo."

Maj is annoyed. "And *I* imagine? That this mansion of yours will be poorly constructed because you never pay attention to the details of anything, and it will fall over and you will be crushed in a mountain of glass and diamonds and wood ... and ponies."

Kallan is outraged. "*MOM!* Maj just said that I was going to be crushed and killed!"

"Yes, well you did say she was going to be a homeless poo-eating beggar."

"That's true."

There is a short silence, and then Maj says darkly, "Don't think I've forgotten about the teeny-head thing, because I have not forgotten. This is going to go down as one of my childhood-destroying moments."

"Making a list, are you?" I ask.

"More like an inventory ... a giant inventory of your failings," Maj informs me.

"Wait, I thought this was about Daddy."

"Oh, he's in there, but if the list was a book and had a title, it would be something like "**ALL THE TIMES MOTHER HAS FAILED ME AND ALSO A FEW TIMES DADDY MESSED UP**, by Maj Wehrmeister.""

Mark laughs and raises his glass to toast Maj's book. She looks at him disdainfully. "Not even, Daddy."

Mark waves the waitress over and orders two more beers.

Maj is apoplectic. "**ARE YOU KIDDING ME RIGHT NOW? ANOTHER BEER? WHO IS GOING TO DRIVE ME HOME? WHO HAS BEEN DESIGNATED TO DELIVER ME SAFELY TO MY HOUSE? WHO IS THE SOBER ONE IN THIS FAMILY? THERE SHOULD ALWAYS BE A SOBER ONE! HOW DOES THIS FAMILY NOT KNOW**

THAT THERE SHOULD ALWAYS BE A SOBER ONE?"

"Someday," Mark informs Maj as he waves weakly to the people whose attention has been drawn by Maj's outburst, "You are going to make someone a super fun and teeny-headed girlfriend."

I point at Mark accusingly. "Maj! Put that in the notebook! That's soul-crushing, that's what that is."

Maj is speechless.

Kallan leaps into the silence. "The other day, Mom? I saw this woman while we were at Target. She had two little girls and a cart filled with stuff. I watched her, and she just kept holding things up and asking if her daughters liked stuff, and then she would throw the things in the cart. Anything her daughters brought her, she just kept letting them throw stuff in the cart."

"This woman sounds brain-damaged."

Kallan reaches to rest a hand on my forearm. "She just kept plucking things off the racks and buying them, Mom. It was amazing! She just kept plucking things!" She sighs. "Why can't you be plucky like that, Mom?"

"Because I am not an idiot?"

"Hmmmph ... I'm being serious! I want a plucky mom."

My second beer arrives, and I take a drink. "I will try to be pluckier, Kallan."

"You mean you will buy me stuff I ask for?"

"Nope, I mean that I will strive to be braver and more cheerful when faced with mothering adversity."

She bounces in irritation. "Remember when we were home-schooling, and you used to make us lists of vocabulary words?"

"Yes."

"I meant to tell you how ANNOYING that was."

I lean over the table to ruffle her hair. "I adore and worship you, my beloved progeny."

She wriggles free, "STOP VOCABULARYING ME!"

Our food arrives. Maj says, as she checks to be sure her chicken is cooked thoroughly, "I just have a few more thoughts about your alcohol intake, Mother."

I wave an angry hand in her face. "Nope. That's enough out of you. Your father and I are each having two beers with dinner. We are your parents and we are responsible adults. So you hush up. Don't say one more rude thing." I stare into her eyes in challenge. "Suck in the rude, Maj. Whatever those next words were going to be, just suck them right back in."

"Mother, I am simply expressing my opinion regarding your unfitness to parent in this moment."

I grit my teeth. "Suck ... in ... the ... rude."

In response, Maj inhales with a huge and exaggerated sucking sound, and promptly chokes on her own spit. As she coughs and gasps for breath, she manages to shriek, **"I AM CHOKING ON MY OWN SUCK!"**

"Well, there's something you don't hear every day," Mark observes mildly.

"ISN'T ANYONE GOING TO ASK IF I AM ALRIGHT? BECAUSE I AM POSSIBLY NOT ALRIGHT! I AM POSSIBLY DYING OF SUCK RIGHT NOW!"

I take a bite of my salad. "You OK, Maj?"

"IT DOESN'T COUNT AS CONCERN IF IT IS SPOKEN THROUGH A MOUTHFUL OF LEAFY GREENS! HOW DO YOU NOT KNOW THIS? HAVE YOU READ NO PARENTING BOOKS? HOW HAVE I BEEN ENTRUSTED

TO YOUR CARE? I COULD BE DYING!"

"Are you dying? You have a lot of words for someone who might be dying."

"MOTHER, I COULD HAVE BEEN KILLED BY MY RUDE-SUCK AND YOU DO NOT EVEN CARE!"

"That's because I'm drunk, Maj. I'm all cavalier about my children's well-being."

Kallan giggles.

Maj takes a deep breath. **"AND I SAY TO YOU AGAIN ... I COULD HAVE DIED."**

Kallan has a new topic of conversation. "Know what I have noticed?"

"What's that?"

"At school ... in the cafeteria ... you can tell how popular people are by where they sit in the cafeteria. It's like there are unwritten rules that everyone just seems to know." She explains, "I was just thinking about how often our family gets put in the booth by the kitchen or the bathroom. Something about our family screams unpopularity as we walk in the front door, I think."

Maj is aghast. **"THEY GIVE US THE BAD SEATS ON PURPOSE? I WILL NOT STAND FOR THIS MISTREATMENT. GET SOMEONE OVER HERE IMMEDIATELY WITH THE POWER TO ADDRESS THESE ACCUSATIONS! ALSO WHERE IS THE MALT VINEGAR I REQUESTED? LOOK AT ME, WAITRESS WOMAN! WHAT IS WRONG WITH THIS PICTURE? THAT'S RIGHT ... I AM THE GIRL WITH TATER TOTS AND NO VINEGAR IT'S A DISGRACE!"**

Mark sighs. "Yes, something about our family screams unpopularity as we walk into the restaurant. I wonder what that screaming something could be?"

"I KNOW YOU ARE NOT SUGGESTING THAT I AM DRAGGING THIS FAMILY DOWN THE POPULARITY PYRAMID, DADDY. I KNOW THAT'S NOT WHAT YOU MEANT TO SAY."

Kallan is annoyed to have had her topic dragged off course. "Anyway ... Mom, do you have a pen?" I dig in my purse for a pen, and Kallan proceeds to draw a detailed map of the school cafeteria, laying out the tables and explaining the level of popularity assigned to each of them. "There's some overlap, but basically ... over here are the insanely popular kids ... like the kids who live in houses on the lake. Over here are the insanely gorgeous people. Over here are the kids who are popular because they are really good at a sport. Over here are the kids into music. Over here are the teacher's pets. Over here are the troublemakers. Over here are the kids who think it's cool to belong to the Math Club. And then there's this table here ... that's where the kids who don't even understand about popularity at all sit ... the ones who are so unpopular they don't even know there is a thing called popularity to be had. No one who knows anything sits there."

Maj leans to examine the drawing, and she asks her sister, "I don't have the same lunch period as you. Where do you sit?"

Kallan points to a table in the middle of the drawing. "I'm here ... somewhere in the middle with the people who can do impressions and sometimes hide in the bathroom instead of going to class."

I stab an interrupting finger into the drawing. "Wait, what?"

Kallan puts a finger to her lips. "Shhhh ... I'm talking to Maj." She turns back to Maj. "Where do you sit?"

Maj points, her face grim, at the table where, according to her sister, no one who knows anything about popularity would sit. "There."

Kallan looks at her sister and then scrunches up the drawing. "Huh. Everything must be the opposite during your lunch period."

Maj is annoyed. **"I'M DONE WITH THIS WHOLE FAMILY.**

YOU ANNOY ME, EACH AND EVERY ONE OF YOU."

There is a moment of collective silence, and then Mark says, his voice dreamy, "You know what we should do? We should get a boat."

I am incredulous. "The four of us on a boat? Are you insane?"

Maj nods knowingly. "I told you he was drunk."

Kallan reaches to take his glass from his hand. "Seriously, Daddy. A boat? We would kill each other."

Mark laughs. "Right? It would be amazing!"

Maj raises her hand. **"YOUNG LADY WITH THE NAME-TAG OF ANNABELLE WHO IS GETTING PAID TO SERVE MY NEEDS WHAT I WANT TO KNOW IS WHERE IS THE MALT VINEGAR?"**

Kallan turns to her father. "Alright, Daddy. Here's the deal. I am willing to support you against Mom's impressive powers of No-ness in this boat dream if you are willing to talk about the possibility of a pony."

No-ness?

Mark shrugs, as though there is no problem whatsoever. "The pony can live on the boat!"

Maj waves her hands in surrender. "So we're getting a boat. That's just great, because we are clearly a family who should have a boat. First day out on the river, I predict we are all kicked to our drowning deaths by the pony."

I raise my glass to Maj's. "Good one, babe!"

She looks at me disdainfully. "Not even, Mother."

So long, suckah

Mark left early this morning, and he was gone before the girls got up.

They don't notice he is gone at first. They eat breakfast, get dressed, fix their beds, pack their backpacks. And then Kallan starts wandering aimlessly around the house calling, ***"Daddy! Daddy! Daddy!"***

And then they both appear before me, and Maj says, "What did you do with Daddy?"

I sip my coffee. "What did I ***do*** with him? Nothing."

"We can't find him. What happened to him?"

"What do you mean, what ***happened*** to him? He had stuff to do. He left a while ago."

Maj looks at me suspiciously. "No one told us that."

Kallan nods her head in shared sister outrage. "Yeah! No one told us he was leaving."

"Daddy and I do not always check in with you guys when we make our plans for the day. Stunning news, I know."

They sit on the couch across from me, stare at me as I drink my coffee and check my text messages.

Maj speaks thoughtfully, "Remember that time I woke up and our cat was gone? And you told me that he had gotten confused and climbed in another lady's car? A car that looked like ours but wasn't ours? And then you said he liked it so much at the other lady's house he decided to live there? Remember that?"

"Yes, but Maj? You were like two and a half! How do **you** remember that?"

"It's not the cat I remember so much as the **lie**. Because he didn't get in some nice lady's car at all. You gave him away and then lied to me about it."

"Ummmmm ... sorry?"

"Just how dumb did you think I was, Mother? Cats don't get in cars."

Kallan speaks up, "Why didn't you just tell Maj the cat was going to the farm? That's what they do in books all the time. The pet who won't behave? Or who gets all sick and is going to die? Suddenly the parents tell the kids the pet went to the farm and is all happy living at the farm. Kids in books are stupid."

Both girls stare at me. I think for a second before responding. "OK, listen. I don't usually lie to you guys, but I thought Maj would be upset at the news I had given the cat away. So I lied. I could have told her the farm lie, but I told her the cat-loving-stranger-in-a-car lie. This was nine **years** ago. Geez."

Maj turns to her sister. "You know why we had to give away my cat? Because it wouldn't stop peeing on you."

Kallan's eyes are huge. "WHAT?"

I interrupt, "That is actually true. The cat hated you from the moment we brought you home. It didn't actually pee **on** you, but it did pee all over everything you owned."

They think about this for a moment in silence as I head to the kitchen to pour a second cup of coffee.

"Hey, Mother?"

"Yes, Maj?"

"Where *is* Daddy, anyway?"

"He's at a conference."

"Where, though? Where is he?"

"I don't know. He said something about a farm."

"That is *not* funny, Mother!"

Kallan snorts and giggles in the background. "Yeah, Maj! Mom lured Daddy into the car with coffee and banana bread and then drove him to the farm while we were sleeping!"

I giggle. "Daddy will be happy there, Maj ... he has fields to run around in and animal friends to play with and all the hay he can eat."

Kallan is delighted at the image. "It wasn't fair to keep him cooped up in the house all the time. It's better this way."

Maj is exasperated. ***"YOU GUYS THINK YOU ARE FUNNY, BUT YOU ARE SO NOT FUNNY. I JUST WANT TO KNOW WHERE DADDY'S MEETING IS! WHY IS THAT SO HARD?"***

I wipe away tears. "Sorry, babe ... the conference is in Portland."

Maj shrugs her backpack onto her shoulder and waits at the door for Kallan to tie her shoes.

Kallan is still giggling. "Can't you just see it, Maj? Mom drives Daddy out to the farm, and he's drinking his coffee and eating snacks all happy, and then she opens the door right next to the barn and she kicks him out."

Maj is crabby. "Would you stop? Mother, make her stop."

"Wait, Maj, listen! Mommy kicks him out and then she drives away and she yells out the window ... *So long, suckah!*"

I am destroyed. I can't even breathe I am laughing so hard. I manage to gasp out, *"So long, suckah?"*

Even Maj is giggling now, although she does gather enough breath to tell her sister, "You are not allowed to say sucker. That is a bad word."

Kallan turns inquiring raised eyebrows to me. "I can't say **suckah**?"

"It's not the worst word, but it's not a word you can use everywhere."

"So I have to choose my moments?"

"Yup."

Maj looks at me all seriously as she opens the door. "Daddy will be home when we get home, right?"

"Yeah, he'll be home."

Kallan giggles again, "Unless he gets confused and goes home with some nice lady in a car that looks like ours."

She runs off. Maj stays to stare into my eyes. "He'll be home, right?"

"Yes, Maj. He'll be home."

"Promise?"

"I promise."

And then they are both gone, and I am here with my dogs and my coffee and silence.

Well, not actually silence, because there is still giggling.

So long, suckah!

Oh my god.

New sister attitude

The four of us are settled on the couches of the living room. I'm reading a book; Kallan is flipping through a fashion magazine; Mark is checking his phone; the dogs are settled at our feet. Maj looks around suspiciously. "This looks like a family meeting."

I look up from my book. "What?"

"This looks like a family meeting. This feels just like the moment right before someone tells me everything is going to change."

Mark looks up as well. "Summer is coming. That will be different."

Maj eyes him. "But we're staying here? We're not moving again?"

"Yes. We're staying here."

Kallan asks, "Can we take swimming lessons at the lake this summer?"

I nod. "Sure."

Kallan returns to her magazine.

Maj persists. "Nothing big is happening? Just summer?"

"Just summer."

"OK, then." She thinks for a minute. "What about that boat-thing Daddy mentioned? Are we getting a boat?"

Mark answers, "Probably not this summer, but yes ... at some point, I would like to get a boat."

Maj looks at me, and I say, "I am not totally on board with the boat thing, but we'll see."

Without looking up, Kallan says, "If we get a boat, you should probably be totally on board or you will drown, Mom."

I laugh. "Good one, Kallan."

Maj cautiously relaxes into the couch. "So the plan for the coming months is just to be calm?"

"Doesn't that sound nice?"

She wrings her hands. "I can't do calm! **WHAT IF THE SUMMER COMES AND IT IS FILLED WITH CALM AND I CAN'T DO CALM AND I DIE?**"

"That would be a bummer."

"BUMMER? THE CALMING DEATH OF YOUR FIRST-BORN CHILD WOULD BE A BUMMER, MOTHER? IS THAT WHAT YOU JUST SAID?"

"Maj, no summer with you is ever calm."

"IS THAT AN INSULT? IS THAT A COMPLIMENT? WHAT AM I SUPPOSED TO DO WITH THAT INFORMATION? WHAT DOES THAT MEAN?"

"It means there is no way in the world you will ever die from calm, Maj."

Maj considers this for a second. "So I'm safe?"

Still without looking up from her magazine, Kallan says, "Well, as safe as one can be with me as a sister."

"YOU ARE NOT ALLOWED TO MAKE ME SPEND MY SUMMER IN FEAR, KALLAN. I WILL NOT HAVE IT AND IT WILL NOT BE SO."

Kallan flips a page. "Maj, you're too easy. I can make you scream in two words."

"NOT EVEN, BECAUSE YOU KNOW WHAT I AM? I AM UNFLAPPABLE. THAT'S WHAT I AM, KALLAN. NO TWO WORDS YOU COULD EVER THINK TO SAY TOGETHER CAN SHAKE ME BECAUSE UNFLAPPABILITY IS MY NEW SISTER ATTITUDE. YOUR WORDS HOLD NO POWER OVER ME, BECAUSE I CANNOT BE FLAPPED."

Kallan holds up one finger, "toothbrush," and then another finger, "toilet."

"AIIEIEIEIIEIEIEIEIEIEIEIEEEEEEEEE!"

And they're off.

A few more words from me

If you enjoyed **Fightball: Dying of Suck**, stay tuned, because I am currently working on the next installment in the **Fightball** series, tentatively titled **Fightball: Lady of Mangle**.

What can you do to help?

Tell everyone you know how much you love Fightball: Dying of Suck!

In fact, if you have a moment, tell some strangers as well — stop by Amazon and write a short review. Seriously. Please do that. It would mean the world to me.

Visit my blog at *www.PrettyAllTrue.com* and check out my posts.

Follow me on Twitter at *@PrettyAllTrue* or on Facebook at *Pretty All True.*

If you have thoughts or suggestions or stories of your own, feel free to email me at *kris@prettyalltrue.com* ... I will respond, possibly at great length. I have a penchant for the last word and all the words that come before.

As for me ... I am Kris. I live in Lake Oswego, Oregon with my husband Mark and our two daughters Maj and Kallan.

They are occasionally exactly as I portray them.

Kris

Also by Kris Wehrmeister

Hope Lies in Less

(a darkly intimate collection of short stories)

CPSIA information can be obtained
at www.ICGtesting.com
Printed in the USA
FFOW02n1338171115
18744FF